ON THE ICE

GRETCHEN LEGLER

# ON *the*

MILKWEED EDITIONS

# ICE

AN INTIMATE PORTRAIT OF LIFE
AT MCMURDO STATION, ANTARCTICA

Published 2005 by Milkweed Editions
Printed in the United States of America
Cover design and map by Brad Norr Design
Inset front cover and back cover photos by
  Gretchen Legler
Author photo by Jennifer Baum
Interior design by Percolator
The text of this book is set in Warnock Pro.
  06  07  08  09    5  4  3  2
*First Edition*

Milkweed Editions, a nonprofit publisher,
gratefully acknowledges support from
Anonymous; Emilie and Henry Buchwald;
Bush Foundation; Patrick and Aimee Butler
Family Foundation; Cargill Value Investment;
Timothy and Tara Clark Family Charitable
Fund; Dougherty Family Foundation; Ecolab
Foundation; General Mills Foundation;
Kathleen Jones; D. K. Light; McKnight
Foundation; a grant from the Minnesota State
Arts Board, through an appropriation by the
Minnesota State Legislature; a grant from the
National Endowment for the Arts, and private
funders; Sheila C. Morgan; Laura Jane Musser
Fund; an award from the National Endowment
for the Arts, which believes that a great nation
deserves great art; Navarre Corporation;
Debbie Reynolds; Cynthia and Stephen Snyder;
St. Paul Travelers Foundation; Ellen and
Sheldon Sturgis; Surdna Foundation; Target
Foundation; Gertrude Sexton Thompson

Charitable Trust (George R. A. Johnson,
Trustee); James R. Thorpe Foundation; Toro
Foundation; Weyerhaeuser Family Foundation;
and Xcel Energy Foundation.

Library of Congress
Cataloging-in-Publication Data

Legler, Gretchen.
On the ice : an intimate portrait of life at
McMurdo Station, Antarctica / Gretchen
Legler.—1st ed.
    p. cm.
ISBN-13: 978-1-57131-282-2
(pbk. : acid-free paper)
ISBN-10: 1-57131-282-X
(pbk. : acid-free paper)
1. Legler, Gretchen—Homes and haunts—
    Antarctica—McMurdo Station.
2. Authors, American—Homes and haunts—
    Antarctica—McMurdo Station.
3. McMurdo Station (Antarctica)—
    Social life and customs.
4. Authors, American—20th century—
    Biography.
5. McMurdo Station (Antarctica)—Biography.
I. Title.
PS3562.E39Z47 2005
814'.54—dc22
                                    2005023103

This book is printed on acid-free paper.

# ON THE ICE

# ACKNOWLEDGMENTS

I am grateful to the National Science Foundation Artists and Writers Program, and its now retired director, Guy Guthridge, for providing me and other writers and artists the opportunity to go to Antarctica, and for having made my time there easy, productive, and exhilarating. Thank you to all those at McMurdo and elsewhere on that icy continent who lent me their time and shared their humor and their stories. Over the years it took to complete this book, many individuals and organizations helped provide space and time for research and writing, including residencies at Hedgebrook, UCross, and Norcroft; the excellent reference librarians at the Scott Polar Research Institute in Cambridge, England, who helped me through the Institute's incredible collection of articles, maps, diaries, artifacts, and pictures of Antarctica; and travel assistance and other support from the two universities at which I have been employed—the University of Alaska Anchorage and the University of Maine at Farmington. Most of all, I want to acknowledge the invaluable help of so many wise and talented writing friends and mentors, from Alaska, Maine, and other far-flung parts, who took the time to read drafts of this manuscript and to comment and suggest changes. The process of creating this book was an arduous, but immensely pleasant and satisfying one, thanks to all of you. Finally, gratitude to H. Emerson Blake at Milkweed Editions, whose enthusiasm and precise, imaginative skills as an editor made the final stages of shaping this book a wonderful experience.

Several chapters of this book previously appeared in other forms as essays or prose poems in the following magazines, journals, and books: "Nacreous Clouds," in the *Sandy River Review*, Spring 2005; part II of "An Antarctic Quintet" as "Walking," in *Going Alone: Women's Adventures in the Wild*, Susan Fox Rogers, ed. Seattle: Seal Press, 2004; "The Sky, the Earth, the Sea, the Soul," in *Eco-Man: New Perspectives on Masculinity and Nature*, Mark Allister, ed. Charlottesville: University of Virginia Press, 2004; "An Antarctic Quintet" as "Moments of Being: An Antarctic Quintet," in *The Georgia Review*, Winter 2002; part V of "An Antarctic Quintet," as "Pole," in *Orion*, Winter 2000; "Southpole" and part III of "An Antarctic Quintet" as "Sounds," in *The Women's Review of Books*, November, 1999; and part I of "An Antarctic Quintet" as "The Blue," in *The Antarctic Sun Times*, December, 1997.

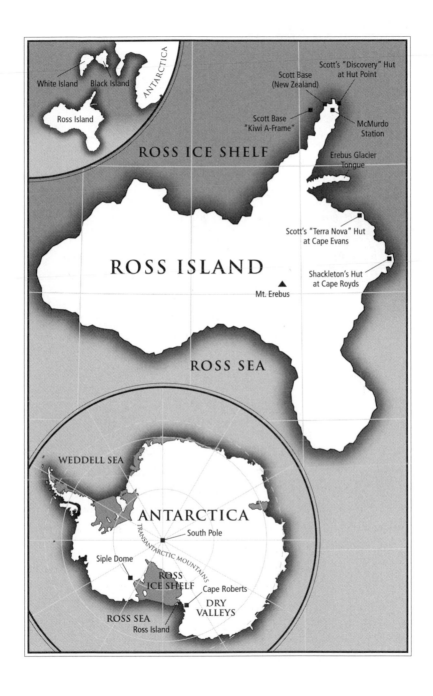

White Island   Black Island

ANTARCTICA

Ross Island

ROSS ICE SHELF

Scott Base
(New Zealand)

Scott's "Discovery" Hut
at Hut Point

Scott Base
"Kiwi A-Frame"

McMurdo
Station

Erebus Glacier
Tongue

ROSS ISLAND

Scott's "Terra Nova" Hut
at Cape Evans

Shackleton's Hut
at Cape Royds

Mt. Erebus

ROSS SEA

WEDDELL SEA

ANTARCTICA

South Pole

TRANSANTARCTIC MOUNTAINS

Siple Dome

ROSS
ICE SHELF

Cape Roberts

DRY
VALLEYS

ROSS SEA

Ross Island

# ARRIVAL

## BENDING INTO THE WIND

McMurdo Station's Chapel of the Snows is a tiny church, painted powder blue and white, with a petite, steepled bell tower, something you might expect to see on a hill in rural New Hampshire, with cows grazing nearby, but here it is framed by the gritty utilitarianism of the main United States scientific base in Antarctica. It sits perched on a dark dirt mound at the edge of town, its unlikely backdrop a barren, sweeping plain of ice and the far-off dark arc of the Transantarctic Mountains. In this vast landscape of ice, dirt, and stone the chapel sits daintily, seeming distinctly out of place, making one look twice and blink—as forlorn and slightly comic as a hotdog stand on the moon. At once amusing and sacred, the stained glass window inside the church depicts a host, a chalice, grapes, wheat stalks, a Bible, and a penguin—all on a background the shape of the continent of Antarctica. The parishioners here are called The Frozen Chosen.

The Chapel of the Snows is where I spent part of my first Sunday at McMurdo Station, having touched down in Antarctica only a day or two before, still stunned by its hardness, and still humbled by the knowledge of its distance from everywhere else I had ever lived. Antarctica! I'd been set down in a place that was so alien, it might as well have been another planet. I was experiencing, like many who'd traveled here before me, an exhilarating and disturbing sense of unease, and the chapel provided a place to sit and contemplate what might lie ahead for me—what awakenings might be in store, what challenges, what discoveries—both as a writer and as a person. During the service a lay minister read from the *Song of Solomon* to celebrate the end of the Antarctic winter. "Listen! My lover! . . . See! The winter is past; the rains are over and gone." The light was returning—not yet a sun, but a buttery glow around the edge of the horizon, like the low rays of a hidden fire. Even this premature possibility of sun, I heard later, was enough to make some of McMurdo's winter-over residents weep with joy.

McMurdo Station itself has the rough stuck-together feel of an old military installation, a remote oil company drilling site, a frontier mining camp, and a college campus blended into one, with its drab-colored, squat administrative buildings; its brown high-rise, steel-sided dormitories; its rough, unpainted plywood sheds; its mammoth silver fuel tanks; its battered, olive green canvas jamesways; its crisscrossing webs of electrical wires; its storage lots dotted with tarp-covered cargo; its dry, pebbly roads and walkways; its gleaming, modern laboratory buildings; the smell of diesel fuel, and the steady hum of engines. It offers no frills. Its simple dirt roads are navigated by orange pickup trucks, snowmobiles, bulldozers, and rambling figures swathed in nylon and fur. It has a beleaguered, tough working-person's look, as would any human habitation in any similarly extreme land. The town, in all its thin, wind-blasted glory, is built on Ross Island at the edge of the Ross Ice Shelf, approximately 78 degrees south, nearly at the bottom of the world. Out beyond

McMurdo spreads the frozen Ross Sea, and farther out still lie the mountains, which in late August explode with orange and pink and yellow light. High behind the town looms the volcano, Erebus, rising 12,000 feet above sea level, a great smoking mound of white.

I arrived in Antarctica in late August, at the end of the Antarctic winter. It is during this two-week period—called Win-Fly, for Winter Fly-in—that a seasonal window opens in the tempest of storms, cold, and darkness of the Antarctic winter, allowing a few early planes to land at McMurdo. Win-Fly offers winter-over residents of McMurdo, for the first time since the station's closure to the outside world the previous February, the promise of new faces, fresh fruit, and real mail from home. In the six months between February and August, the 150 people stationed at McMurdo survive with no mail, no flights from New Zealand to bring fresh food, no newcomers, just each other and the long Antarctic winter darkness. During Win-Fly the new arrivals include a handful of early scientists, some replacements for winter-over workers, and a few of the army of administrators who will run McMurdo, the larger science camps scattered here and there over the continent, and the United States' Amundsen-Scott base at the South Pole come summer. After the two-week flying period is over, no additional flights arrive in McMurdo until October, when the official science season begins and hundreds of scientists and summer workers come to the ice, swelling McMurdo's population to a thousand or more.

I journeyed to the ice not as a scientist, nor as any kind of technician or tradesperson, but as a writer. I'd flown to Antarctica from another place that seems equally far away and wild in the minds of many: from Alaska, where I'd been teaching writing at the University of Alaska in Anchorage. I'd traveled from one pole to another; from the top to the bottom of the world. I was in Antarctica under the auspices of the National Science Foundation's Artists and Writers

Program, which gives artists a chance to do what scientists have done since the beginning of Antarctic exploration—tell the story of this land, try their hand at making some human sense of its vastness and its terrible beauty.

The artist's job, my job, would be to bring back visions, to translate that which could not be communicated in the language of numbers. I'd spent several years of my life as a journalist, and I planned to use those skills and talents—a deep sense of curiosity, an ability to listen, a certain agility with words—to talk to the people who dwelled and worked in Antarctica, to find out about their lives, and to listen to their stories about themselves and this icy place. Besides the stories of people, I also wanted stories of the land itself. I planned to talk to scientists, too, to go with them and explore, and to see for myself what Antarctica was made of. I felt deep down that to be grounded in the world I had to be connected to land—what American writer Henry David Thoreau called "hard matter in its home." I wanted to know about the "hard matter" of this mysterious land, this place so few had been to and which so few understood. I was armed with notebooks, a computer, pens, and cameras and eager to begin. What was Antarctica made of? What did it look like? What did it mean?

I was drawn to Antarctica mostly by curiosity and a hunger to see new places and things. Since childhood it had been my nature to explore. I would don my biologist father's bush jackets and pith helmets and stalk about the yard with binoculars and a butterfly net, leading my little sister on a search for the source of the Nile in our suburban Utah neighborhood. My first thirst for Antarctica had come when, at a writing retreat in northern Minnesota, I discovered in the eclectic library of the elderly gentleman upon whose island the retreat was located, a copy of Robert Falcon Scott's last journal. I could see Scott then, shivering and miserable in his tent amid a howling Antarctic storm, scribbling out his last words: "For God's sake, look after our people." The bleakness and threat of the landscape he wrote of appealed to me. It was unlike any place I'd ever been or imagined.

Scott and the others who explored Antarctica had, like me, adventurism in their blood, and were, also like me, just plain curious. They'd been eager to risk their lives for their countries, in order to establish claims in honor of England, in honor of Norway. That era of nationalism was long gone, but I had other equally compelling personal reasons for wanting to go to Antarctica. In addition to my professional journey, I had, as did Scott and the others, I'm sure, intimate reasons for wanting to travel so far from the beaten path; reasons that were never publicly revealed in the times of those earlier explorers, and perhaps weren't even discussed in private. I wanted to embark upon not only a journey of physical exploration and discovery of new lands, but also an exploration of inner worlds—places in my own heart and mind where I might find some respite from the relentless judgments I passed upon myself and others, places where I might be able to lay down burdens of resentment I'd carried so long, places where the unappreciated flesh and desires of my body might find themselves at home, places that I hoped being so far from my ordinary self would help me find.

My arrival in Antarctica was both startling and mundane. For five hours I'd been cramped with seventy-one others into the cargo hold of a U.S. Navy Starlifter, being carried across the ocean from the greenness, spring humidity, and cherry blossoms of Christchurch, New Zealand, to the bleak cold of this strange new world. On the plane with me were scientists who would study such things as penguins, the ocean floor, seals, and the ozone hole. There were also janitors, plumbers, electricians, carpenters, and other skilled tradespeople who would provide the services needed to make McMurdo Station function. Snacking from paper sacks full of sandwiches, candy bars, and fruit given to us as we boarded the plane, we all looked alike, all swathed in thick black wind pants or quilted canvas overalls, voluminous red parkas, white insulated boots, mittens, and hats; all buckled tightly into the rows of seats made of red nylon webbing; all hypnotized by the cold in the long, gray steel belly of the plane and by the soporific roar of the engines.

As we neared the Ross Ice Shelf, the pilot ordered us to prepare ourselves for landing. We zipped our parkas, tightened down our fur-ruffed hoods, and pulled on the bear-paw gauntlets, face masks, goggles, and balaclavas that were part of the forty-five pounds of Extreme Cold Weather gear we'd been issued at the staging center in Christchurch. We landed as softly as any regular passenger plane at any airport, gently setting down on McMurdo's Pegasus runway, built on an ice sheet several hundred feet thick. The plane door fell open, the wind rushed in, and the already cold cabin grew bitterly colder. Outside, it was at least seventy degrees below zero Fahrenheit, so cold the air burned my lungs, sucking the warmth out with a seemingly audible *whoosh!* The scene was a chaos of parka-swaddled bodies and swirling snow. We moved in a cold fog, drifting into a big red bus called Ivan the Terra Bus, which then lumbered slowly over the ice toward McMurdo Station. In the bus, with the heater on, we began to peel back layers of clothing. The windows frosted over. I scraped a hole in the thick white rime, the crystals flying up and melting, ticklingly cool, against my face. I peered out onto the moonlike landscape rolling by. Where on Earth, if on Earth, had we landed?

Mesmerizing white was all I could see at first, as if the whole bus was enveloped in a cloud. Then around the edges of the white the sky began to glow pink and peach and gold. The pale spring light of Antarctica hung low along the horizon. Snow sifted eerily over the ice, blowing in its own confused directions. It was a desert of ice. A solid sea. An endless plain of wind-sculpted snow. In the distance was the volcano, Erebus, with its plume of smoke and steam lazily rising into the gold sky. And then we were in McMurdo: a little dirt- and ice-covered village, smelling of diesel fuel, the rumble of the station's power plant beating out a cadence in the dry, cold air.

Ross Island, the site of McMurdo Station, is itself a mere speck compared to the vastness of the Antarctic continent—Earth's last "new" land. It is a continent that was not even officially sighted until well into the nineteenth century, having until then only been guessed at, named first by the Greeks *Terra Australis Incognita*, the unknown southern land. Early reasoning suggested that since there was a land mass at the northern pole of the earth (or so they believed—the north pole actually is ice only in the winter, melting to water during the summer), there must also be a land mass at the southern pole, though no one had actually seen such a thing. The continent represented a great gap in the world's map until whalers first sighted land and then set foot on the continent. Explorers then finally started drawing in the lines, eventually learning indisputably that what Captain Cook, in his voyage around the Antarctic Circle in the 1700s, had proved wasn't there, actually was—in all its hulking, icy magnificence. Antarctica did exist!

Originally mythic, Antarctica remains so today, a fantasy tabula rasa, or blank slate, a "white lantern" at the bottom of the world—a land yet to be entirely mapped and named, a land not yet officially owned or governed by any nation. The metaphorical possibilities of this whiteness, this newness, have not been lost on those who go there. Artists, scientists, explorers, and politicians have all vied to be the first to write upon the symbolic fresh page of Antarctica. They have wanted, these men and women, by brilliance, by technology, by sheer will, to make their mark, to extract their riches, to test themselves against the ferociousness and mystery of the land, against the very idea of the unknown—to bend it, to be bent by it, or to be broken.

The troubled, passionate human past of Antarctica was so immediately and heartbreakingly present to me upon my arrival, with Robert Falcon Scott's abandoned hut within a stone's throw from the room where I would sleep. Scott, a British Navy man who tried twice to reach the South Pole, was just one of Antarctica's early explorers, but the one with the most famously tragic story. He raced to the South Pole, in his second bid to get there, against Norway's Roald Amundsen, arriving only weeks after the Norwegian. There was no comfort for him upon reaching the pole, only grief. "Great God, this is an awful place," he wrote. It was made even worse, he added, by his having gone all that way without the reward of being first. He then perished on his return, just miles from a supply cache, in a tent in a howling storm, where he wrote out final letters to loved ones and expedition supporters, ending one such letter with those terrible words begging that the families of the dead be properly cared for: "For God's sake, look after our people."

It was with both reverence and a certain amount of cynicism that I considered Scott and the other supposed heroes of his age. Their missions were so pumped up by myths of Victorian masculinity and national pride; they were so trapped by their arrogant notions of what constituted honor, so keen to worship science as the only worthy way of knowing. They dragged their shiploads full of England to this place where England didn't matter, and tried to paint their version of the world onto this canopy of white. But at the same time, their efforts inspired awe. The stories of their hardship and deprivation, told in numerous explorers' tales, are sorrowful and often dreadful. What compelled them to come here, to try over and over to get to the South Pole, to cross the continent against such odds? What made them choose such a path, such a goal, and then to consciously pursue it? It was such labor, such effort; it was so cold! Was it faith that compelled them, or bullheadedness, or folly, or all three? Did they start out as fools and die that way, or were those who lived shaped and strengthened by Antarctica as steel under a hot hammer, coming out more alive and more wise? Did Antarctica teach them something that it could also teach me?

Those early explorers, in their straw-filled, hobnailed boots, their canvas and wool clothing, their hoosh mugs and heavy reindeer sleeping bags, had to have been supremely hearty to survive in Antarctica, I thought. They had to have been stronger than their physical bodies would allow. If you look at photographs of these early expeditions you don't see burly he-men who look as if they could bully their way through anything. Instead, you see men who look small and regular, like men you know, in rumpled dirty clothes with funny hats and frost-bitten faces. If it wasn't their physical brutishness that got them through, then surely they must have had some kind of special spiritual assistance or some kind of mysterious inner strength—or maybe not. Maybe they were *normal*. Maybe they *did* just have faith—faith that their endeavor was worthy, that *they themselves* were worthy, that they would succeed, or not, and that all would be right, somehow, in the end.

At the Sunday service in the Chapel of the Snows, where I sat enfolded among a dozen others, protected momentarily from the cold, the ice, and the wind, the lay minister read to us about light and love and beginnings: "Listen! My Lover! Look! Here he comes leaping across the mountains, bounding over the hills. My lover is like a gazelle or a young stag. Look! . . . My lover spoke and said to me, 'Arise My Darling, my beautiful one, and come with me. See! The winter is past; the rains are over and gone. Flowers appear on the earth; the season of singing has come, the cooing of doves is heard in our land.'"

The light was a lover beckoning the sleeping planet to arise and come out into spring, beckoning the sleeping heart to come to love. It was hopeful, promising something rough and new. I imagined the dark winter that was just done, what it must have been like finally to have it over, to see the sun all pink up against the sides of Mount Discovery. I imagined what the winter had been like, with the stars and the moon and the aurora australis and the biting, numbing cold. I imagined how it might have felt to be so isolated, and then to have the sunrise, to have new people come, to have bananas and oranges, fresh milk and cheese, to have a letter from home signed with a solid mark from a longed for hand.

In my dormitory room later, I knelt on the thin, narrow bed with its institutional sheets, ribbed bedspread, and scratchy military wool blankets, and gazed out the window. Below my window McMurdo's power plant hummed and buzzed and growled. Telephone and electric poles stretched their wires across what otherwise would have been an unobstructed view toward the distant, clear Transantarctic Mountains, the Royal Society Range, Mount Lister, Mount Discovery. The mountains lay directly distant, across miles and miles of flat, frozen sea ice. They rose out there, jagged and bathed in delicate pink light. There was just that: flatness, space, whiteness, rising up to spectacular mountains. Later in the season, I would be able to look out onto the windswept ice and see the tiny black dots of seals basking, a dark line of waddling emperor penguins come from the open sea, an orange pickup truck, another huge gray airplane come to deliver more scientists or supplies. But for now, early in the season, it was only this achingly beautiful prairie of ice.

These were the mountains that the early explorers had to cross to reach the Pole; mountains that stood between them and their dreams, them and the center; mountains that ran like a jagged backbone from the Ross Ice Shelf on one side of the continent to the Ronne Ice Shelf on the other; mountains that separated East Antarctica from West Antarctica; mountains full of glaciers and crevasses, full of the frozen bodies of dead explorers, the petrified ponies and wrecked sleds and abandoned supplies of the Age of Heroes.

To my right ran a crushed lava road leading down to Scott's Discovery hut. Come January, the area I could see, called Winter Quarters Bay, where Scott parked his first boat, the *Discovery*, in 1902, would become McMurdo's ice pier, at which various ships would dock, including the supply boat the Green Wave—a boat that would bring McMurdo its once-a-year resupply of everything from cigarettes to automatic teller machines. From my window I could clearly see the hut and the cross on the hill beyond it; Vince's Cross, a memorial for one of Scott's men who had slipped and fallen on that very slope, tumbling into the Ross Sea.

Later in my stay, on the bad windy days at McMurdo, when temperatures reached -100°F and the winds were up to 40 knots, friends and I would pretend we were Scott and his men, bending into the wind, our shoulders to the gale, trudging along from our dorm rooms to the galley or to the science lab, as if we were hauling those enormous sleds across the ice, up over the mountains to the plateau and on to the great center, the Pole. The wind would send bits of dirt and ice stinging by our faces, and our goggles fogged as we tried to breathe in the coldness. Ice formed on the outsides of our fleece neck gaiters. The wind was so strong we could let ourselves fall into it with all our weight and were held upright by the strength of it. We curved ourselves into the wind, taking one clumsy step at a time. It was enough to make you cry, or laugh, or both—at the futility, the naïveté, the arrogance of those old explorers' efforts, but also at the human spirit—all that struggling with forces over which you had no control, trudging forward with some fantastic goal in your heart.

# TWO HUTS

From the outside, Robert Falcon Scott's Discovery hut looked cheery and neat—all tidy and shipshape, with sharp corners, weathered wood, and little blue-tinted windows. It looked like a place where you could be perfectly comfortable and warm, huddled around a stove with a mug of cocoa in your hands, listening to a story, watching the snow fall. But, said my friend Tom Learned as we stood at the door, this was no dream house—it was more like a nightmare.

The Discovery hut had one of the saddest histories of all the huts built in Antarctica by early explorers. Tom, a manager at McMurdo Station, had made a hobby of studying and photographing the huts, and he'd offered on this day to take me and a new friend, Ruth Hill, a McMurdo electrician, on a tour. Within easy walking distance of McMurdo, the hut was prone to frequent visits, and care had been taken to control access by keeping it locked, although a key could be checked out and an escort provided. Many of the early explorers' huts in Antarctica had been ransacked by souvenir hunters, and efforts by the Antarctic Heritage Trust, a New Zealand–based group, were under way to catalog what was still left in the huts, repair those that were in derelict condition, and put out a worldwide recall for scavenged items.

Under the eaves outside the hut, atop a pile of frozen canvas, lay a mummified seal. Whoever hauled it up from the cold sea only several hundred feet away probably was going to cut it up and boil it for blubber but never got around to it, and now, almost a hundred years later, there it still lay.

Tom knocked before he unlocked the door and slid the bolt back. "Knock, Knock. Honey, I'm home. Oh no, not blubber again!" he laughed, his joke putting us at ease but also making my spine prickle, as if to speak aloud here was an invitation for a curse. We climbed over a snowdrift in the doorway. On the wall in the entryway the snow had blown into delicate sculpted patterns. Frost crystals sparkled on the ceiling. The walls were black from smoke.

"Smell the blubber in the air?" Tom asked. We put our noses to the air and sniffed. It smelled cold, dank, dusty, and thickly fishy.

The hut, used well by expeditions over many years, had never provided the kind of welcoming security that its sturdy wooden shell seemed to promise. Scott's men had anchored their ship in Winter Quarters Bay right next to the hut, but lived in the ship itself during the winter of their first journey in 1902. The hut they primarily used for storage and as a place to put on plays. It was put together from prefabricated materials bought in Australia, in the design of an early Australian squatter's hut. Scott used the hut again for camping out and for storage when he came back for another try at the Pole in 1910, the trip from which he did not return.

The Discovery hut was also used temporarily by Ernest Shackleton's men in 1908. Scott remarked upon returning to the hut in 1910 that it had been left a mess by his then rival, and that Shackleton's men hadn't had the civility even to close the doors and windows properly. The hut was also inhabited for a winter by members of the Ross Sea party of Shackleton's later Transantarctic Expedition in 1914. The tale of the Ross Sea party has its own chapter in the disturbingly tragic story of Antarctic exploration.

Shackleton was to start his trek to the South Pole from the Weddell Sea, on the other side of the continent, while the Ross Sea party was to start near McMurdo, with a main base at Cape Evans, laying depots of supplies every sixty miles over the 1,561-mile path from Ross Island to the Beardmore glacier, so that Shackleton would have food and gear for the last leg of the journey. But things went wrong, as they always seemed to in Antarctic exploration: the Ross Sea party's ship, the *Aurora*, broke its anchor and floated away, and the sledging parties got separated from one another, with part of the group marooned at the Discovery hut, cut off from their comrades thirteen miles away at Cape Evans by unstable sea ice, impassable glaciers, and darkness.

"Bleak" is how Tom described their five months in the hut. "Grim" is how one expedition member, Dick Richards, put it, no doubt understating the true nature of things: "We found the hut a grim place for the next five months." They were already starving (a day of food near the end consisted of eight lumps of sugar and half a biscuit), already suffering from scurvy and frostbite, already thick with filth from not bathing for more than a year, and the hut, which was woefully inadequate for the cold and storms of winter, offered little haven. While five members of the Ross Sea party huddled there, they were unaware that on the other side of the continent Shackleton's ship, the *Endurance*, had been stuck in the ice, to be crushed and abandoned, leading to one of the most fantastic boat journeys of all time, as Shackleton and a few of his men sailed in the *James Caird*, a twenty-two-foot lifeboat, from Antarctica across the Drake Passage to a whaling station at South Georgia island, where they got the help that would save the rest of the expedition members.

Under the best circumstances Discovery hut never got above freezing. It was so cold that the men piled up crates and covered them with blankets, trying to create a smaller space around the stove so they could keep warm. They even started tearing down the hut itself for fuel to burn. It disturbed me to think of it; men—civilized, educated British gentlemen—like a pack of desperate dogs, ripping at the wood of the hut, slowly demolishing the very edifice that offered them any hope at all of survival. They slept like dogs, in a big pile on a wooden palette on the floor—all five huddled together for warmth. They carved seals and boiled them and used the blubber for light and also for food. In the rusting frying pan atop the rusting stove lay desiccated pieces of blubber. In a pile near the door lay hunks and slices of blubber and the backbones of seals, piled up, waiting to be eaten or boiled, everything so long frozen that it seemed more like stone than flesh.

"Blubber was everything," Tom explained. "Everything." It was this reduction that moved me, that haunted me; human beings reduced by force and circumstance to blubber, to instinct, to the body. All but two members of the Ross Sea party who were marooned at Discovery hut eventually made it back to join companions at Cape Evans, walking safely across the sea ice in July, once the sea had frozen, and were rescued in 1917. The two unlucky ones died when they tried to leave the hut too early in the season, before the sea ice was safe for walking.

Crates and tins of all sorts and sizes still littered the hut, detritus from at least four expeditions, abandoned all. Ruth and I walked around in the dim, cold light, our feet soft on the lightly snow-covered wooden floor, looking at and touching these relics. Piled on shelves were blue and orange Huntley & Palmers Biscuits tins; tins of Bird's Baking Powder and Fry's Cocoa; handmade lamps from cut-up tin cans in which the men had burned blubber, with a piece of cloth for a wick. There was an old hardware catalog; a can labeled Beach's Golden Plums; a big box that had written on its side "Captain Scott's Antarctic Expedition 1910—Homelight lamp oil."

The men of all these adventures had come to take what they wanted from a place that offered nearly nothing—no gold, no timber, no spices or other riches, no peoples to enslave—only the fun of being on adventure with other men, and the honor of being first, for

England, for Norway, for mankind. Of course there was knowledge, too—science—which is its own kind of riches—facts about rocks and ice, knowledge of what the wild land *looks* like, knowledge of what is there. They created maps and charts; they named things—all of which produced something of value—not only stories, but also a kind of permit or stamp of ownership. The place then belonged to them, in a way. But only in story. Only in their tales and maps. It's remarkable that more art didn't come out of those early expeditions, given how educated these men were, how literate. They were all poets in those days. It was almost as if the early explorers left their imaginations behind and took only their rational selves, their hero selves, their patriotic selves, limiting any intimate personal insight or poetic epiphany to a few guilty lines in a notebook or in a letter to a loved one.

When it was time to go, in their disappointment, they left so many ghosts behind. You could feel it in the air. It was true of most of the old Antarctic huts. There was a sense in them of spaces suddenly vacated, not a feeling that the occupants had planned to leave, then packed their bags carefully and departed, but that they'd instantly fled, fled for their lives, leaving not only food and equipment behind, but something else alive and haunting; dinner half cooked, rumpled clothing, unmade beds, photographs, personal things, and some part of their very souls.

Like many girls and boys, I'd been keen as a child to discover secret, remote places—nooks high up in trees, quiet spots at the back of closets, holes in hillsides, pine-surrounded spots in forests—where I could create fantasy worlds; places where I would dreamily sing nonsense songs and putter or read, where I could imagine myself an explorer or anything else I wanted to be. The dreaminess about place had followed me into adulthood, where it asserted itself with both more subtlety and more urgency—it was partly a need for shelter, a yearning for home, a place to safely settle and pull life in close around me. I wondered as we toured Scott's hut how you might go about making such a place into a home—warming it up so that the ice melted, creating light, cooking some fragrant stew on the woodstove, scrubbing it clean, making it a place of shelter and intimacy. Or was this place already too full of ghosts?

On my way out of Scott's hut I noticed a slab of blubber hanging on a nail from a shelf. "Why is that there?" I asked Tom, hoping there might be some shred of domestic logic to it—that was how they hung blubber to cure before they fried it, or some such thing. But the logic had more to do with fear and carelessness than anything else. "That," he said, "was just the last place they threw it on their way out." How much would I, if I'd been one of them, have cared, or not cared, about anything else but salvation come rescue time, come time when a ship to fetch me pulled up in Winter Quarters Bay? Would I, too, have simply jumped up, abandoning my turned-over chair in my hurry to get out, not even closing the door?

Ernest Shackleton's hut at Cape Royds was not unlike Scott's Discovery hut at Winter Quarters Bay. It was made of the same kind of wood, now so weathered by years of storms that it was gray and showing signs of the wood itself being scoured away from its grain. It was similar to Scott's hut in its simple design with sharp, neat corners. As with the other huts I visited there were piles of ancient supplies left inside and out—rusted-open cans spilling out white beans, rice, oatmeal, dried peas. Like the other huts, it also had been built to house expeditioners as they prepared to launch their effort at the Pole. But, for all it had in common with the other huts, this one felt different. No one had died here, no one had frozen to death. There was an absence of despair.

Shackleton and his men built the hut at Cape Royds in 1908. His was called the Nimrod Expedition. On this trek, Shackleton got to within ninety-seven miles of the South Pole, closer than anyone before him. In this hut Shackleton and his expedition members passed their Antarctic winter preparing for their journey and also creating *Aurora Australis,* a book of poems, essays, and stories. Produced in limited numbers for expedition members, it included a fantastical interview with a life-size emperor penguin who spoke with a Scottish brogue and a nightwatchman's tale about the dreamy, intimate musings and fantasies of the sleeping men around him.

Shackleton, historians say, was a peculiar man in that, although he publicly advertised that his ambition was to reach the Pole, secretly he wished for only one thing—to be in Antarctica. He loved Antarctica, as a place. It was for him the place in which he felt most at home. He died of a heart attack at the age of forty-seven, in 1922, onboard his ship the *Quest* as it waited in South Georgia for another trip to the Antarctic. He'd been eager once again to be on the ice. After coming down with some kind of chill, he directed his final words at his expedition mate A. H. Macklin, who'd admonished him to take it easy, "You are always wanting me to give up something. What do you want me to give up now?" He was buried in South Georgia at the request of his wife, Emily, who said she could not bear the idea of him in a claustrophobic British cemetery. He'd once written to her, "Sometimes I think I am no good at anything but being away in the wilds just with men." He would never reach the Pole. He would lose no men to heroic deaths on that icy continent. Yet, he became a hero. Shackleton is widely regarded as an excellent leader, someone who had the ability to convey successfully to others his belief that ordinary people were capable of heroism, of endurance beyond their own imagining.

Antarctic historians and scholars have remarked that, for many early explorers, Antarctica was an idea more than an actual place, a landscape of the mind. That may be why so many of those early expeditions resulted in death and misery; men went unprepared for what was actually there, and many became heroes for their foolishness. Shackleton recognized the metaphorical resonance of his journeys to this wild, white continent, but seemed not to be dazzled by the language of nationalism and science. More than any other explorer, it seems, Shackleton loved Antarctica for what it was—its hard matter—its rocks and ice. He loved it simply, in the way that a boy or girl might love the woods and want to be there among the trees and birds at any chance.

Shackleton's hut lay near an Adélie penguin rookery. On the day I visited it, with Ruth and McMurdo's ice expert, Buck Tilley, the sea ice had opened up to a point just below Cape Royds, and the air was full of the sounds of Adélie penguins chattering and quaking, the sounds of seals mewing and lowing from the edge of the ice, and the trumpeting sounds of emperor penguins, which walked comically about on the ice below, sometimes upright and sometimes dropping to their bellies and speeding along with the help of their feet and flippers. The penguin colony and the hut lay atop a hilly rise, one side of which fell with rocky steepness to the ocean, and another side that sloped gently down to a still frozen part of the sea. From a distance, one would not have been able to tell that the scattered black dots on the icy slope were penguins, they blended so well into the muted colors of the scene. Up close the penguins were in constant motion—waddling to and fro, squawking, pecking, fluffing themselves, building their neat rounded nests from piles of marble-sized volcanic pebbles, stealing pebbles from their neighbors, while, with their backs turned, they were being stolen from in return. The scene was a wild fantasy of a fecund, teeming, primal animal Eden. Everywhere there was noise, movement, life!

Among the items inside Shackleton's Cape Royds hut that intrigued me most were the cans and bottles of food, particularly the tall, thin-necked bottles of gooseberries, still wrapped in golden straw and capped with wax plugs. The bottles were about twelve inches high and tapered toward the top. The straw shone with the thin light that came in one of the few windows in the hut. Where the straw was parted I could see inside the clear bottles the deep purple—so purple they were almost black—gooseberries. They were small and round, suspended in dark purple syrup. The bottles of gooseberries stood on a table in a nook at the back of the hut, behind the huge iron woodstove, along with cans of curried rabbit, mulligatawny stew, minced collops, and parsnips.

With their gay color and certain sweetness, the gooseberries must have been a kind of memento vivere—a reminder, amidst all the hardness and chill and ice of this continent, of the pleasures of living. I'm sure there was a reason Shackleton brought the gooseberries, beyond the fact that they were beautiful. To prevent scurvy, perhaps. But to me they signified a carefulness, an attention to detail, that pointed toward a confident and calm character behind it all; someone who knew who he was, where he was, and why; someone who felt most at home in one of the harshest landscapes on the planet. I tried to imagine what dishes might be made with the gooseberries, why they were packed with straw, whether they were sweet, what it might have been like, in 1908, to open such a bottle and have the pleasure of eating them, spilling them over porridge or cooking them in a pancake, all that rich purple pouring out. There was a big difference, I thought, between a home, even one in as unlikely a place as Antarctica, and a cold, deliberate, barely sufficient shelter.

# ANTARCTIC TIME

Antarctica, scientists say, hasn't always been one huge chunk of ice and stone, although it's difficult to imagine this land being anything else. From the science camp at Cape Roberts, on the edge of Granite Harbor, a long helicopter ride from McMurdo Station across the sea ice and up along the coast of Victoria Land, you can see the rough, rocky shore of the continent rising high and fast from the frozen sea. You can see where glaciers make their infinitesimal progress, spilling down from the Polar Plateau into the now solid ocean. You can see the hundred-foot-high icebergs loom, lavender and turquoise, leaning against one another as if to help support each other's weight. At their bases seals gather. The landscape seems monstrous, beautiful, and frozen for all time.

Time is exactly what is being studied at Cape Roberts. Big Time. The scientists at Cape Roberts want to pull up meters and meters of muddy, gooey earth from the ocean bottom in hopes that this ocean floor sediment will tell them a story, a story that started 100 million years ago and ended in a period called the Oligocene epoch, a relatively "young" period in Antarctica's history—stretching from about 36 million years ago to about 23 million years ago. During that time, Antarctica's climate is thought to have begun to change from warm to cold—from a climate that supported green plants and trees, to one of wild wind and ice, where only microscopic creatures could survive the deathly cold. The tubes of mud from the ocean bottom at Cape Roberts were to be analyzed for everything, including pollen, sea creatures, minerals, and evidence of tectonic activity, giving scientists a better idea of what the climate might have been like during the Oligocene, and, by extrapolation, more information about how major climate change happens in general.

As you enter the camp, just in front of the colorful array of blue, red, and yellow buildings, a signpost lists the various distances to the home countries of the scientists at work here: London 16,914 km; Rome, 15,850 km; Berlin, 17,005 km; Canberra, 3,782 km; Christchurch, 3,707 km; Washington, 14,703 km. Home is a long way away for all of us. On this windy night, we're all sitting around in the nylon tube-hut that is the galley at Cape Roberts, part of a cluster of hard-sided and nylon-sided huts that include sleeping quarters, storage, a kitchen, a workshop, an ablutions block with hot showers and toilets, and a science building. The nylon is a good barrier between us and the wind and cold outside. We're sitting comfortably, me and perhaps ten of the men working on this project, having had a fine dinner made by the cook in his cramped but well-equipped kitchen at the end of the multiple rows of tables. There were vegetables, meats, fresh breads, cookies, hot drinks, and we're relaxed and warm and everyone seems companionable. The men around me are woolly-bearded and bright-eyed. Many have the look of utter physical exhaustion in their slumped bodies and splayed legs, having been at it all day at the camp's drill site, some distance away over the ice. Their brown denim coveralls are caked with mud.

Someone jokes that he can imagine people coming to this site two million years from now and drilling down to find the past, just as these men have been doing today, but instead of coming up with mud and the shells of ancient sea creatures, the new drillers would cut through the engine block of a giant excavating machine. They laugh. It amuses them to think of someone from the far future drilling into the distant past and finding our present. The men get into a good-natured argument about time and stuff—*things*—and about what's junk and what's not. Now, the *things* in Robert Falcon Scott's Cape Evans hut are "historical rubbish" says Cape Roberts project manager Jim Cowie.

"They're *picking up* every piece of our rubbish now; soon there'll be no history!" says another.

"There's a point at which it all becomes historical, I suppose," says yet another.

A final voice interjects, "It's still just rubbish," and they laugh.

Back in the olden days in Antarctica, says Cowie, in the mood to reminisce, the place was full of junk and no one seemed to mind. McMurdo Station and nearby Scott Base, where the New Zealanders lived, were awash in booze and rampant with wastefulness. In McMurdo alone there were thirty bars. He remembered one day when the U.S. Navy pilots stationed at McMurdo accidentally thawed all their stored frozen food. They were threatening to throw out full boxes of steaks, pork roasts, and chicken breasts. The New Zealanders took advantage of situations like that, Cowie says, salvaging the meat for their sled dogs, which have since been banned from Antarctica, for fear they would pollute the environment with their feces, and also because of the difficulty of feeding them. Scavengers the Kiwis were, Cowie laughed, making raids on McMurdo from time to time to collect items such as engines that were about to be dumped into Winter Quarters Bay, or other useful things that otherwise might have been set fire to in the McMurdo dump, which would go up in billowing, smoky flames once a week or so. For their part of the mayhem, the New Zealanders slaughtered seals that came to bask at the shoreline near their base for "tucker" for their sled dogs.

It all came to a big end in the late 1980s when Greenpeace, the international environmental organization, rolled into town. They had their reporter in downtown McMurdo sticking microphones in people's faces, a direct satellite linkup to the world. Now, everything is different, says Cowie, a New Zealander who came south as a mountaineer when he was twenty-four years old, and is astonished at the impeccable organization of the project that is currently camped at Cape Roberts. Everything is in order, from marmalade to toilet paper.

While we're sitting in the galley, Peter Barrett, the scientist in charge of the Cape Roberts project, comes back into the room. Barrett, perhaps six feet tall, gangly, with a gray mop of hair and a boyish cowlick, is lean and pleasant, a gentleman scientist of an old school. He's rubbing his left ear, which is red from his being on the phone for nearly an hour, talking with scientists in McMurdo who've been studying the samples the drillers at Cape Roberts have been hauling up from beneath the ice and water.

"Well," he says, in a droll, New Zealand accent, "there's apparently more resistance to the Oligocene age than I appreciated," and the room erupts with laughter. Some of the scientists at McMurdo think the first samples of mud might be older than thirty-four million years and some think they might be much younger, and this matters *very* much. Current theories about global warming suggest that if Antarctica melts, it being the repository of 90 percent of the world's ice and 70 percent of the world's fresh water, sea levels would rise globally, creating reefs and underwater obstacles out of what is now dry land, people's homes, cities. In the United States, for instance, such a rise would flood all of Florida and most of Louisiana, parts of all the other eastern seaboard states, a crescent of Texas along the Gulf, and bits of the West Coast. What scientists find out at Cape

Roberts and at other sites in Antarctica where climate change is being studied will help create a history of the Antarctic ice sheet's fluctuations and thereby help predict the future.

"This isn't going to cause some schism in the geologic community, this stuff that we're drilling, is it, Peter?" Cowie asks.

"The nature of geologic inquiry is that positions have to be taken and defended before it all comes together in one glorious harmonious whole," he replies, with a poker face. They all laugh again. Barrett tells the crew sitting around the tables that the bigwigs are coming tomorrow to check things out.

"Are they bringing their own boxing gloves or do I need to supply those?" Cowie asks.

In the big scheme of things, the Oligocene, the period of time Peter Barrett and others at Cape Roberts hoped to study in the samples of mud from the bottom of the Ross Sea, is fairly recent history; it is postdinosaur time, prehuman time, pretty much squat in the middle of the Tertiary period when the earth began to take on the "modern" appearance it has for us today. The earth itself is about 4,600 million years old. We've been here, in the shape of *Australopithecus*—the first "near humans"—for about 5 million years, in the shape of *homo erectus* for about 1.5 million, and as *homo sapiens* for about 100,000. Not long at all. The mammals that are familiar to us today began to appear during the Tertiary period, when most of the modern families, genera, and species came into existence. According to one artist's depiction, during the Oligocene, the Victoria Coast of Antarctica, the site for the Cape Roberts drilling project, looked somewhat like many parts of Alaska look today—the massive Ferrar glacier filled with temperate glacier ice, carrying sediment to a vast outwash plane and sea; open water filled with icebergs from calving tidewater glaciers; and beech forests established in scattered enclaves along the coast.

When Barrett said there was more resistance to the Oligocene than he appreciated, what he meant was that some of the scientists—namely, the "pollen people," who were disagreeing with the paleontologists—thought the samples might be reflecting things that happened as far back as seventy million years ago, on the boundary of the Cretaceous and the Tertiary periods, referred to as the K-T boundary, the time of large dinosaur extinction we know so well. ("We may be drilling in dino land," said one scientist.) Some, however, thought the core was much younger than the Oligocene, instead coming from about 2 million years ago, during the late Pliocene epoch.

Disagreement over the age of these tubes of earth from the bottom of McMurdo Sound could generally be drawn along already well-established lines—between what are called the dynamicists and the stablists. The stablists think that Antarctica became covered with ice about fifteen million years ago and has remained that way. The dynamicists think it was most recently glaciated only two million years ago and that over time the ice sheet has melted and reformed many times, in other words, that the ice sheet is dynamic, and that the melting and reforming happened relatively quickly in terms of geologic time. The stablists think climate change happens slowly. The dynamicists think it can happen catastrophically; that in the space of a geologic minute, New York could become the new lost underwater city of Atlantis.

Although the project had been impeccably planned, funded, and staffed and was newly under way, already generating heated interest and debate, bets on whether it would actually succeed were still out. The carefully written planning manual for the Cape Roberts project included this caveat: "Now for a cautionary word. Antarctic fieldwork has always carried risks due to weather and mechanical failure and this project is no exception. . . . Thus we are facing some uncertainty." Despite the uncertainty, Barrett had proceeded with the project, hot for it to get under way, and hopeful that the ice in McMurdo Sound would hold. It was a crapshoot, a gamble—the other players being weather and time.

Uncertainty is always a key player in Antarctica. The place encourages, indeed demands, a different kind of relationship with weather and time. It requires an acquiescence, rather than a relationship of struggle. In fact, Antarctica is the unalloyed opposite of the culture of immediacy in which most Americans and Western Europeans live at the beginning of the twenty-first century. "Antarctic time" is what those who've worked on the ice call it. It makes Antarctica tick, this time that is not like other time, this time that is radically indifferent to human desire or need, that proceeds of its own ancient accord.

"Throw the clock out the window, we're on Antarctic time," laughed one McMurdo carpenter as he described an experience "hot-bunkin' it" (rotating in and out of a single bed, the sheets still hot from the previous sleeper as the next exhausted laborer climbed in) as he and others strove to complete a project on Antarctica's Black Island. Time, the kind of time you look at your watch for confirmation of, the kind of time you look to the horizon or the angle of light for confirmation of, quite simply did not matter to the carpenters and engineers installing the satellite dish at Black Island. The day went beating on, brilliant and searing as the sudden white of a lightning flash. And the work never stopped. *Could take two weeks, could take a year, but probably two weeks*, might be the typical response of an Antarctic worker asked to assess the time span for a task. This isn't laziness, but an almost Zenlike suppleness that seems necessary if one is to survive the gritty difficulties of work in such an extreme environment. You are not in control. *You bend.* Or you break.

Antarctic time is as close as I've ever been to *kairos* time, the flip side of *chronos*. *Kairos* is by origin an ancient Greek term meaning the "right or opportune moment," but has also come to designate a certain quality of time. *Chronos* is the kind of time we most often live in—the time of the calendar and the clock, the time of must and quick and before-its-too-late, minute-grabbing time, the time one sees advertised on television that can be "saved" by purchasing a new cell-phone or item of wrinkly-free clothing. *Kairos* is time not measured by the clock—big time, eternal time, sacred time, the time of creation, the time of myth and wisdom—more like Antarctic time.

Geologist Peter Webb, one of the chief scientists directing the Cape Roberts project, came to Antarctica in 1957, during the IGY, or International Geophysical Year, which brought scientists from all over the world to Antarctica. Webb is a man who appreciates Antarctic time. He's been doing research in Antarctica nearly all his adult life, and he finds it a salvation, an environment where people can recover their ability to think. "When I leave L.A. I slip a few gears. When I get to New Zealand I slip a few more, and when I get here I slip a few more," Webb says, describing the striptease nature of his journey from Ohio State University to the West Coast and beyond, as he makes his way to McMurdo Station, arriving lightly clad, as it were, having shed the garments of his other life. This is a place, he says, where airplane flights can be canceled and rescheduled for a day to two days later, as if it didn't matter, which, in Antarctica, it doesn't.

Despite the hubbub of science at McMurdo, Webb says, this is a place to relax and explore things, where you have time to explore them in a much more logical and much less aggressive fashion than you would in any other setting. The freedom scientists feel from time, finally unleashed and able to work at a more befitting pace, translates into more congeniality as well, Webb has noticed. Among scientists, there is greater freedom to disagree. At home, Webb remarks, "I do sound-bite thinking. I do little wee thinking. You even find yourself doing many small things because you can't do one big thing!" But down here, he adds, "It's dead easy to think big twenty-four hours a day."

The hyperacceleration of time and the way it seems to have compressed not just our physical lives but our imaginations as well, is not just a mirage, not just a *feeling*, it is a reality. It has to do with something illustrated well by Moore's law, which states that the number of components that can fit on a microchip increases exponentially about every eighteen months. (This has been happening since 1959.) That means it doubles, then doubles again, and again, and again, each double doubling itself the next time over, providing us tinier and tinier and still tinier and faster computers, more and more powerful microchips, and in the process creating a veritable technological wall, where the rate of increase is going straight up, like a rocket into space. Technology and the pace of it is what drives the economies of the developed nations of the world, and therefore shapes our sense of value and time.

In these western economies we feel everything must move at the speed at which technology moves, creating a culture of immediate gratification, a culture that has deeply changed the old-fashioned sense our nineteenth-century ancestors might have had of space and time, of postponement, of waiting. We live in a world where speed is the paramount virtue. The chilling thing about it all is that *natural* patterns and cycles are happening, moseying along, ambling, shambling, scuffling away, at the same pace they always have—at the same snail's pace that they occurred in the Jurassic, the Oligocene, the Pleistocene—being measured in millions of years. Humans still move arithmetically—one, two, three, four—not exponentially. And so we become, fundamentally, out of sync, out of time, at odds with the movement of the natural, ancient world around us—the world of glaciers, of tides, of sun, moon, stars, and even our own hearts. We respond to this feeling of being at odds with time by trying to *force* time, make time do *our* bidding.

When I discovered the possibility of going to Antarctica, it seemed, in addition to being a lifelong dream and a momentous professional opportunity for a nonfiction writer, a chance to stop the clock, or turn it back somehow and start anew. It seemed possibly a place where I wouldn't be burdened by the same patterns of sky, of thought, of action, that I paced through daily in my ordinary life; a place that might lend me some much-needed perspective; a place where, like Peter Webb, I could think in bigger terms about my life. I needed to travel. I needed to get out of town, out of the country, off the continent. I needed, a friend told me before I left, to see myself anew, and it might not be easy. "You're going to be face-to-face with yourself; you'll be a different person when you return," she had said. If that was true, who would I be? My life was not peaceful, it was true, not sustaining. It seemed haunted by unfulfilled desires, filled with ghosts and obsessions, old hatreds and buried hurts—yearnings for love, for acceptance, from others, and most crucially, from myself.

Shortly before I left for Antarctica I had two painful dreams. In one I went to visit my parents and found their house entirely bare, echoing hollowly. I wandered heartbroken and confused through the barren rooms, wondering why they'd gone, and where, whether they'd died, or moved and not told me, whether they'd known I was coming and were hiding. They were just . . . gone, and the house was sterile and achingly empty.

My sister, a year younger than me, committed suicide when she was in her early twenties, a tragedy that ripped the already thin and frayed fabric of my family into shreds. In the yawning dark of that event, I saw truths about myself, my siblings, and our parents that angered . . . and saddened me. What saddened me most was that I saw how frozen we'd all been, how unable we were to express to one another the most basic, the most common, of emotions—joy, love, fear, grief. I was afraid that I would never learn how to do this—how to make the connection between my body and my self, how to let my body express its truths in its own graceful, wild language of tenderness, tears, and laughter. I was afraid I'd never thaw, never come alive.

In the other dream I was skiing down a winding slope and glided past a wolf sitting in the middle of the trail, its black fur thick, its eyes bright and cold with wildness. My skis still pointing downhill, my hair flying out behind me, I yelled excitedly over my shoulder to my sister, who in the dream was skillfully negotiating the thin forest-lined trail. I'd seen a wolf and I was unafraid, treating the sighting as something rare and wonderful. But soon more and more wolves began to appear along the trail and in the forest, running along beside me, keeping pace, their eyes matched with mine. Fear caught up to me. For the rest of the dream I searched out wolf puppies, tiny gray furry things, and one by one I wrung their necks so violently that their heads came off in my hands.

It had been this way for a long time. On the outside I remained anyone's decent definition of a sometimes charming, intelligent, high-functioning ordinary citizen, college professor, friend, lover, taxpayer. On the inside, at my center, was a thinness. In my dreams, I haunted empty houses looking for love and I killed helpless things, perhaps even my own hopes of coming fully alive. At least I had come that far, I reasoned, far enough to recognize the drama in which I was cast, but I hadn't yet let go of my part. I hadn't yet learned to stop living in the past—expecting miracles from parents now too old themselves to parent their grown children, wishing that I could somehow resurrect my sister, or at least come to terms with my helplessness to make right any of the things I felt had led to her death. Sometimes I felt my heart was made of ice. Sometimes I wanted to stay frozen forever. Sometimes I believed that I could force a solution to it all simply through the power of my own will, bending time, bending other people, like a magician bends a spoon with a hot stare.

The samples of sea floor at Cape Roberts come out of the ground looking like what they are—long tubes of dirt and clay, about as big around as a woman's forearm. They're handled as if they were newborn babies, passed through a tiny square window opening into the drill site lab, where they're laid reverently down on a bench (one scientist petted the first cores), looked over first for tectonic markings, sectioned into one-meter lengths, subjected to physical properties tests, cut in half lengthwise, packaged for transport to the Cape Roberts camp, and then photographed.

Half of the core would become the sampling half and the other half would be an archive half sent directly to the Antarctic Research Facility at Florida State University in Tallahassee. The sample half would first go to the laboratory at Cape Roberts and then be shepherded on to McMurdo Station. Along the way the tube of clay, mud, dirt—the millions-of-years-ago past—would be looked at, poked, drawn, photographed, picked at with dental tools, put through magnetic sensing devices, weighed, and then computerized and studied for strength, plant debris, evidence of glacial deposits, effects of deep water current flow, and the presence of certain minerals. In the end it would go into cold storage in Bremerhaven, Germany, and from there the samples of Antarctic time would eventually be made available to scientists worldwide.

The drill site itself is a cacophony of sharp masculine yells, fierce pounding engines, wind, and the sounds of the drill banging, banging, banging, as it bores through the sea ice and into the ocean floor. At the top of the drill pad hover professional drillers, international nomads who do their earth-piercing business all over the globe. They dance about, shifting gears, turning levers, watching like hawks the multitude of gauges and dials. They are tiny, wiry men, adorned with hard hats and ear protectors, filthy and mud-spattered, their faces splotched with gray goo. Below them, in the mud room, stand two men who hardly look like men at all, covered as they are from head to toe in a pink mush that they mix continuously as the coolant/lubricant that keeps the drill bit from damage.

When the first bit of core, real core, not just mud from the surface, came out of the drill, says Brian Reid, one of the bearded, bright-eyed New Zealanders at Cape Roberts, telling a story over tea in the camp's galley—when the first bit of real core came out of that noisy, yellow-engine-pounding room full of small, tight men with hard hats, gloves, and mud-splattered faces, when that first long roll of dark clayey material came up, and when driller Pat "The Rat" Cooper, who's drilled all over the world, when Pat himself brought the core into the drill site lab, people started yelling all around, "He hit the hard stuff, He hit the hard stuff," well, you should have seen it—"Pat and Peter holding it and jumping up and down just like kids, just like kids, just like kids."

But in the end, after about a week of drilling, after the recovery of only 140 meters of core (not the 1,300 meters they'd planned on), the drilling project was shut down for the same reason it had to be postponed the year before, storms in the Ross Sea created swells that weakened the ice, which was only a few meters thick to begin with, and the drill and all the drill site buildings had to be towed to shore before they sank down to lie atop the layers and layers of time at the bottom of the sea. All of Cape Roberts was packed up and everyone went home to try again another year.

How does a person know when to be hard or soft, to be aggressive or not, to push against time or yield to it? In Antarctica, says Webb, you learn it over time. You waste your whole first year on the ice trying to get things done. Peter Barrett agrees: "The people who succeed down here are not 'Time Equals Money' sorts of people." Soon, Webb explains, you learn that nothing works in Antarctica if it's forced. You reach a Tao-like state, where you try to stay at the center of the circle and let things take their course. In the *Tao Te Ching*, Chinese master Lao-tzu reminds patiently that the teachings in his small book are older than the world, and simple. The ordinary person, he says, is always doing things, yet many more things are left to be done. The master does nothing, and so he leaves nothing undone.

In the end you learn how not to fight the system, Webb says. The master shapes events as they come. There is a time for being ahead, a time for being behind. The master does her job and then stops. Every day something is dropped. Less and less do you need to force things. The soft overcomes the hard. The slow overcomes the fast. If we cling to things we create problems. Forcing a project to completion, you ruin what is ripe. The simplest way is the clearest. Things are not really so urgent, the Tao reminds us. When two great forces oppose each other the victory will go to the one who knows how to yield.

# DELICIOUS BURDENS

O n a sign above the kitchen counter in the stark little hut that sat in the midst of the wild flatness of Ross Island's windless bight, along with directions for lighting the diesel stove and the New Zealand oil lamps, called Tilly lamps, was this message: "There are no fun police within four miles of here. There is no excuse for not having fun out here. Have fun!" Four of us—Charlotte, Ruth, Chris, and I—were staying overnight in this Antarctic getaway known as the Kiwi A-Frame, owned and occasionally loaned out to Americans at nearby McMurdo Station by the Kiwis, a nickname for the New Zealanders at Scott Base.

The hut was made of black plywood and sunk low in the snow, in a space carved out by wind and kept clear by shovels. A stovepipe in the roof let go a thin stream of warm smoky air from a fuel-oil stove called a preway. Several red-framed windows looked out on the absolute white of the Ross Ice Shelf upon which the hut sat, about four miles from the Scott Base station and another two from McMurdo.

Nearby the New Zealanders had built a small ski lift; the easy run led down the low slopes of Castle Rock, a craggy monolith that stuck its black head up from the flatness and served as a local landmark.

Like me, Chris, Charlotte, and Ruth were eager for a long weekend "vacation" away from the noise and diesel fumes of McMurdo. This was to be an adventure, an unlikely picnic, a weekend away from the farthest away place in the world.

Ruth had driven me around in her electrician's truck the day before so that we could outfit our small expedition—selecting delicacies such as leaves of basil, hot peppers, and small tomatoes from McMurdo's hydroponic greenhouse, and cruising the shelves of the food room, a warehouse stocked with powdered, dried, and canned foods of all kinds for furnishing field parties. She and I happily went up and down the dusty rows, reaching high on the metal shelves for our favorite pasta, soups, teas, chocolate, cookies, nuts, and condensed milk for coffee.

We rode out to the hut in an orange Spryte, a tracked vehicle that rattled and lurched up the hill toward Castle Rock, stopping on the crest of the ridge above the hut so we could gaze out over the sharp peaks, glaciers, and snowfields that fell down the other side of Ross Island, then rattled and lurched down the near side, depositing us finally at the hut. For the first hour, we four shivered fully dressed in our parkas and boots while the hut warmed up, and then we launched ourselves into preparing a spicy pasta dish for dinner. The fresh food from the greenhouse was its own delicious pleasure.

Charlotte had come to McMurdo to be part of the cleaning staff, from a job in her real life as a social worker. In this she was not unlike the many professionals who give up their status, their suits, their ties, and their desk jobs to work for a season in Antarctica chopping food or shoveling snow. Stocky, dark, with her hair shaved down close, Charlotte was often, she said, mistaken for a man. She told stories of little girls staring at her open-mouthed in grocery stores. "It's all right, dear," she'd say to them kindly, "I'm a woman."

Charlotte alternated between mopping floors, scrubbing toilets, and working in the warm moist McMurdo laundry. She called the town an encampment. "You can call it a town, you can call it a station, you can call it what you want. No matter how you dress it up," she said, an amused snarl in her voice, "it's an *encampment*." Her observations were often acerbic. "We don't know who the hell anyone really is down here," she said one day, with a look of mock paranoia on her face. "How can you tell who anyone is dressed up in these clothes?" by which she meant the parkas, wind pants, and boots that obliterated individuality. If it wasn't for the idiosyncratic hats that people wore, carefully chosen dashes of color and whimsy—wool hats, beaver fur hats, baseball hats, slouchy hats, hats with tassels and hats without—Charlotte's observation would have been almost true. You could also tell who was coming at you in forty-five pounds of parka and boots by their gait and their size and shape. Besides being funny and kind, Charlotte was also one of the sanest people I'd ever met. She had a great grasp of the reality of any given situation. "Never feel guilty," she said, "for being sane."

When he wasn't in Antarctica, Chris lived in Park City, Utah. At McMurdo he was a painter. He was a handsome, tall, dark-eyed young man, a drummer, and a massage therapist who had, during the long winter just over, provided massages for his winter-over companions. His inky black, long hair hung down the sides of his face, except when it was pulled back in a tight ponytail. Whenever I saw Chris, his thin body usually was draped in baggy, paint-spattered coveralls. He was pale and vulnerable looking, like a birch tree. The winter before I arrived, he was voted "the sexiest man at McMurdo." He was a searcher and a question-asker, a worrier. He worried he wouldn't have friends when he got home because he'd been so long away. He worried he'd never find God.

Ruth and I had been introduced by Al Martin, the McMurdo Town Marshal and National Science Foundation representative, as he gave me a town tour early in my stay. Al and I had stopped at every building in McMurdo, including the Heavy Shop—the modified pole shed where McMurdo's trucks and other heavy equipment were fixed and maintained by cold-weather mechanics, where metal was welded, where nut-and-bolt problems were solved. I was ushered into one of the shop's chilly, cavernous rooms, where a small woman in clean blue jeans, a purple fleece vest, round, wire-rimmed glasses, and short black hair was half buried in an electrical cabinet. She extracted herself from the cabinet, smiled, and offered her hand to me. I stared at her for a moment, awkwardly, before I realized we had, in a manner of speaking, met before. I'd been carrying her name in my wallet for nearly a year.

A good friend in Anchorage had met Ruth at the Denver airport nearly a year earlier as Ruth was on her way to Antarctica. My friend Connie was alerted to Ruth's presence when Ruth's steel-toed work boots set off the alarm in the security check. When, during a humorous exchange about the boots, Connie discovered Ruth's destination, she'd secured Ruth's name, along with the encouragement that once I was "on the ice" I must look her up. I'd been worried by reports that Antarctica would be a difficult place to be a woman and that I'd have to be on guard at all times against men who'd manipulate me into service as an "ice wife." So I was relieved to know, as reported by Ruth through Connie, that McMurdo was full of interesting, professional, strong, competent women, and that many of them, like Ruth, were lesbians. In fact, there was a joke: How do you get a date with a woman in Antarctica? Answer: Be one.

Ruth's effortless friendliness attracted me, and others too. People told her things, opened their hearts to her, gave her things. One new friend who was an artist in his life off the ice sketched caricatures of her singing, perched on the edge of a stool, her mouth open in a wide "O," hair falling characteristically over one eye, to be posted as advertisements for her final Antarctic concert. She'd become quite famous, in the tiny winter-over community of McMurdo, for her banjo, her guitar, her mandolin, and her sweet voice. She had the face of a young woman, a boyish face, even—wide, clear brown almond-shaped eyes, a dazzling smile. But along with these markers of youth, there was a spirit in her much older even than her actual forty-one years.

As we ate our dinner in the warmth of the hut on the ice, I asked Chris and Ruth and Charlotte what they'd brought with them to Antarctica to remind them of who they were. What I'd carried to Antarctica for a six-month stay fit into two small duffel bags and a small daypack, all weighing less than a hundred pounds, although I'd also sent five boxes ahead of me. The boxes and bags contained, besides the requisite clothing and personal hygiene items, a stack of pictures of friends, pets, and favorite places, notebooks, film, books of poetry and literature, a small library of Antarctic reference books, a set of dress-up clothes, a stuffed animal, and music. I had more clothes than I would wear, more books than I would read, lotion, shampoo, and soap that would go unused, and at least one picture I'd not yet even put up on the wall—someone I cared about, someone I knew wasn't right for me, but whom I hadn't yet bid farewell. I felt an urge to shed it all, all that junk, all that stuff, all those layers of old self, layers of the past. I'd brought so much that I didn't want or need, out of fear, plain fear. But how is one to know what to pack for such a journey so far from home?

When I put the question to Don Brogan, head of supplies at Mc-Murdo, and a self-described minimalist, he said that the first year he worked on the ice he brought what he was told to bring on the list supplied by Antarctic Support Services: a bathrobe, towels and washcloths, three pants (cotton, heavy twill, denim), three shirts, six pair of socks, eight pair of underwear, small sentimental items . . . the list went on. The next year he brought half as much, the next year he pared down even more. This most recent year he brought a few music CDs and realized he could get along even without those. What he needed, he'd discovered, were the clothes on his back. Everything else he could get from the McMurdo galley or from Skua Central.

Skua Central, a cold shed full of clothes, appliances, books, art supplies, shoes, and more, served as McMurdo's version of a secondhand store, being a place where you could leave behind what you no longer had use for, and fetch whatever you needed, free. Every dorm floor had boxes for initial Skua deposits, which were transferred to larger outside bins, then moved to Skua Central. Most items never made it that far, but were "skuaed" directly from the dorm boxes. All over McMurdo people proudly announced, in reference to a new pair of purple cowboy boots, a bright yellow turtlenecked sweater, a good book, that they'd "Skuaed it!" One of the unwritten rules of skuaing was that anything you got from the pile you had to leave in Antarctica at the end of your stay.

The word *skua* comes from the infamous Antarctic scavenger bird, a relative of the gull, whose population experienced a boom in the years before McMurdo stopped its policy of piling garbage in an open heap. To go "skuaing" at McMurdo was to go looking for treasures and necessities that had shortly before been someone else's excess, someone else's burden. In the end, Don Brogan said, you really didn't need much to survive, even in Antarctica.

Gary Teetzel, an engineer in the Crary Lab at McMurdo, brought, wherever he went, a tiny six-pack cooler that he called his "possibles bag"—a bag full of things that he could possibly need and things he couldn't possibly do without. What he put in the possibles bag changed from time to time, but mostly the contents included a toothbrush, toilet paper, string, and a Swiss army knife. "I carried a cigar in there for a while too," he said. A woman friend had given it to him. She had one also. "We were supposed to meet up and smoke them together." That never happened, so after a while he tossed the cigar. This trip to Antarctica he brought one special extra thing: an antique wooden folding ruler his father had given him. "I brought it just to remind me of my father," he said. "My parents are getting old."

Ruth brought her feather comforter, her musical instruments, and pictures of friends. Charlotte brought her souvenir "P-Town" cap, from the gay and lesbian mecca of Provincetown, Massachusetts, embroidered in rainbow colors with her nickname, Huck. Chris, besides his drum, brought his bottles of aromatic oils, drops of which he placed on the stove, filling the cabin alternately with the smell of lemongrass, rosemary, and sandalwood.

How little could you travel with? How light could you make your burden? It was easy to be jealous of people like Don Brogan who could pare down to bare essentials; men like Gary Teetzel who traveled the world with a tiny bag full of string, a knife, and a toothbrush. Still, even if I'd come to Antarctica with nothing, I'd have brought too much; too many worn out stories about who I was.

I'd called my parents from the airport in Los Angeles, just as I was to board the plane for the first leg of my journey to Antarctica. My father was watching television, my mother said, meaning, in the secret language of our home, he wouldn't be happy about being interrupted. When he finally came to the phone he sounded terse, unfriendly. Why couldn't he have at least faked it, said "Good luck," or "I love you," or "Write as soon as you get to the South Pole"? It was nothing new, this cool exchange—it was just a fresh reminder. I'd carried this lack of connection, this lack of intimacy between my father and me, most of my life. It was one of my deepest wounds. I was beginning to think I'd never be rid of it—that my unconscious self wouldn't let me put this burden down, afraid of the void that would be left in the place of my longing and anger.

When I hung up the phone, I felt more lonely than before I'd called. What good could repeating this scenario possibly be doing me after all these years? Why couldn't I just let go? I might just as well be carrying around bags of rocks, like Robert Falcon Scott on his way back from the Pole. The rocks were, in the end, historians say, one of the things that bogged him down and did him in—all that extra weight—but others have vociferously supported Scott's insistence that the rocks be delivered back to civilization, that they contained invaluable geologic information about the world. They were necessary burdens.

We stayed up late, Chris, Huck, Ruth, and I, telling stories of childhood, stories of ghosts. In the dim hiss of the kerosene lamps, Ruth and Huck both talked about dreams they'd had as children, dreams in which they flew. Both swore that they knew their home cities from the air. Ruth said that as an adult, when she'd flown over Union, New Hampshire, with her then husband, she mysteriously recognized every rooftop, even though she'd never flown over the city before, except in her dreams.

Charlotte confided to us that her Antarctic boss, Leslie, had been visited in her McMurdo dorm room by the ghost of a man who died in Antarctica when his vehicle fell through the ice. Leslie woke one night, saw someone in the chair across the room and thought it was her husband Tom, but realized Tom was in bed next to her. People said, too, that there were ghosts of old Antarctic sled dogs wandering about town. Ruth's McMurdo rock band was named Ghost Dog, a name that emerged after two of the band members, on the same day, separately sighted ghostly black hounds.

Ruth told us about her dreams of a home of her own. She'd spent the better part of her Antarctic winter doing real-estate searches online. She'd found a seventy-five-acre parcel with 3,000 maple taps for $70,000 in Vermont, but didn't buy it. That house reminded her of others she'd also felt strongly compelled to buy, but didn't. "There was a cottage," she told us, "one of a set that had belonged to a defunct Vermont resort, being sold one by one for fifty dollars each to any buyer who could afford to cart them away. I wanted to buy one, set it in the woods, and live in it the rest of my life. I wandered through it. I went in the back door. I fell in love with the rag rugs, the fireplace, the French doors. Coming out on the front porch, I looked up to see the cabin's name on a sign nailed above the door. It said *Ruth!*" The story seemed implausible—to have a home named for you, to have your place in the world so specifically located. "I should have bought it," she said, disappointedly, "but I didn't have any land to put it on, and it would have cost a fortune to move."

No generators hummed. No lights buzzed. There was just the thump of wind at the sides of the building, and us talking, settling into place. Ruth played her guitar. Chris accompanied her on his drum. Charlotte hummed along. I read aloud from Walt Whitman:

> I have perceived that to be with those I like is enough,
> To stop in company with the rest at evening is enough,
> To be surrounded by beautiful curious breathing laughing flesh is
> enough, . . .

> (Still here I carry my old delicious burdens,
> I carry them, men and women, I carry them with me wherever I go,
> I swear it is impossible for me to get rid of them,
> I am filled with them, and I will fill them in return).

The next morning the sun coming up around Mount Erebus was brilliant. I awoke next to Ruth, her dark head having made its way in the night to where my shoulder lay under my down sleeping bag. The bed we lay in, all three of us women, was a nest of vibrant-colored nylon and piles of down and fleece. Everything outside was white, sharp and clean as new paper. We heard Chris walking around outside the cabin, taking pictures from all sides, his boots squeaking in the snow. As we ate a pancake breakfast, the food made Ruth think of New England. "In the spring in Vermont," she said, radiating joy in the telling of the story, "we'd make sugar-on-snow. We'd go up to the mountains and pour maple sap on the fresh snow and eat it."

Ruth and Chris, who'd both been in Antarctica for more than a year and would be leaving soon, talked about what they'd do when they "got out," spinning off into their imaginations, lifting themselves out of Antarctica. "I want to be on a beach somewhere sipping mango juice," Ruth laughed. "I want to be in Vermont in the fall for my birthday, when the trees are ablaze." The last time she'd left Antarctica to fly back home via New Zealand, Ruth said, "I took off my shoes at the airport in Christchurch and walked across the grass, right there." That was what she wanted again, right then, just that, the delicious feel of grass under her bare feet and to see the color green.

What Chris wanted to do when he got home was cook, he said, explaining the dish he'd make, as if he'd made it a thousand times, as if it was part of who he was. "The most important ingredients are ginger and garlic. The next most important are bok choy, then root vegetables such as carrots and parsnips, and then, finally, shiitake mushrooms. Chop the garlic and sauté it in olive oil. Simmer the vegetables. Put in some soy sauce or tamari and the ginger. Start the noodles. You need Udon and buckwheat noodles. While the vegetables simmer, start cutting the bok choy. To do this, stack the leaves, then roll them up and slice them so that you have long strips. Throw the bok choy into the garlic, ginger, vegetable mixture. Put the lid on and let the whole mixture steam for five minutes. You don't want the bok choy to be droopy. When it's really green and warm, throw it in with the noodles." He ended by saying, "I usually eat it out of a bowl that I've made." He cupped his hands as though he were holding the bottom and sides of the bowl, held them there against his belly for a moment, then lay them down again on the table, open in a kind of prayer.

During our last night in the hut on the ice shelf, I'd wandered out before bed to empty my bladder at the "pee flag," the yellow flag on a pole designating the place where you were supposed to urinate, so as not to spoil the snow needed for drinking water. I stood out under the southern stars, my head back in the bright cold, looking for some familiar shining thing.

Restoration of the self requires a strange combination of effort and noneffort; fierce will and acceptance. I thought of Borg Ousland, the Norwegian adventurer who, in 1997, hooked a sail to his skis and let the wind help carry him on his solo journey across the continent, from the Ronne Ice Shelf to McMurdo Station. The wind, which had been the burdensome enemy of Robert Falcon Scott and many other Antarctic explorers, was Ousland's friend. Ousland had developed a relationship with this powerful, killing force, and good had come from it. He did not work against the wind. He did not let it pin him down. He was neither victim of its powers nor heroic conqueror.

I believed in the passion of that spring lover who called to his mate: "Arise My Darling, my beautiful one, and come with me." I believed in love and in beginnings. I had faith that if I kept plodding forward good things would come to me; I would find my way to my self, I would find a way to set down my fears and ghosts; maybe I'd even find a way *through* self to something larger beyond. I didn't know what lay out there in that vast land. And in this, perhaps, I was more like those old and new Antarctic heroes than I wanted to admit. They and I had in common faith in reward for the great labor of effort, whether the effort be man-hauling sleds up the steep ice of the Beardmore glacier, sailing with the wind across the continent, or the different but very real toil of working to bring light to one's inner world.

The door of the hut opened and Ruth came out to join me. We both stared up at the sky. "I don't know any of these stars," she said. "Me either," I said. For some reason, then, I felt a glimmer of openness, a kind of clarity that this vast continent I was standing upon encouraged or allowed. I had a sense that I was good enough as I was, that being, just being, was its own bittersweet, heavy-enough parcel.

# WAY OFF THE FLAGGED ROUTE

In the electrical and plumbing supply warehouse at McMurdo Station, pinned up to one dingy wall and illuminated by the florescent lights buzzing overhead, was a poster of eight different kinds of toast. It was labeled "The second annual Toast Chart." With the months February through October running down the left margin, and the names Mary Elizabeth, Jen S., Dave D., Chase M., and Mark running along the top, the poster charted the "progress" of each of these support workers through their Antarctic winter-over. Each piece of toast was a different shade of brown or a lighter "toast" color. And each illustrated something about that person's state of mind or body as the months wore on. By July, the darkest heart of the Antarctic night, Mary Elizabeth's toast was burned, had jagged edges, and was labeled "Don't Touch Me." Jen S.'s was burned and split in half and read, "Pull it Together!" Dave D.'s was darkly toasted and sported little red devil horns. Chase M.'s read "Amen" and had little angels flying about it, and Mark's was licking a lollipop.

By September, each piece of toast had a clock face marking the hoped for time and date of the person's departure from the ice. Dave D.'s toast clock had the hands turning backwards and read "If time were to go any slower I'd be moving backwards." At the bottom of the chart, across all of October, were Polaroid snapshots of each person, bedraggled, wane, and big-eyed. To be toast, in Antarctic lingo, or to be toasted, meant you were crisp, fried, tired, wrung-out, sick of winter, and ready for some green. By the time you were toast, they said, it was way past time to leave.

The electrical parts warehouse was stop number one on my McMurdo town tour, hosted by the town's supply boss, Don Brogan. An affable, scruffy Texan with a thick middle, Brogan had been employed off the ice as, among other things, a policeman and as director of a veterinary clinic; he answered nearly every question I put to him with cryptic humor. When asked why he was in Antarctica, he replied, "Many a good Antarctic career has been started on a failed relationship!" End of story. Although Brogan wasn't forthcoming with details about his romantic life, on or off the ice, others were. I learned that there were as many configurations of romantic relationships at McMurdo as anywhere—polyamorous lesbians, loyally monogamous heterosexual men and women who came to the ice as married couples and lived that way in their cozy dorm rooms, loyally monogamous gay men who did the same, single men and women looking for life mates or perhaps just pleasant erotic encounters, heartbroken lovers who'd lost their newly-found Antarctic sweetheart to another on-ice suitor. There were also those who at home lived in harmony with their chosen mates and families, but on the ice coupled up with an "ice husband" or "ice wife." Many of these relationships, sometimes with a decade of history behind them, were kept strictly within the bounds of the continent, some secret to the steady spouse at home, and some not.

My tour with Brogan was not my first tour of McMurdo Station, though it may have been the weirdest. These different walks through town reminded me of brochures that advertised walking tours of London—the Bloomsbury literary history walk, the Sherlock Holmes mystery walk, the Jack the Ripper tour. My first McMurdo town tour was courtesy of Town Marshal Al Martin, the National Science Foundation representative in Antarctica. He was indeed actually a town marshal, just like in the old West, and he had a badge and a gun to go along with the title—the only American in Antarctica allowed to have a firearm. He led me through every building at McMurdo, including the town's small and eclectic library. Martin's tour could have been dubbed the "official town tour."

With Brogan, I got the "underbelly tour." He'd promised to show me a different side of McMurdo: its seedy underside of cavernous, neglected warehouses of canned and frozen food, outdated computer equipment, beer and soda pop, paper and pens and sticky notes, copper pipe, hazardous waste, and lightbulbs. While Brogan's tour was of buildings and things, it also proved to be a tour of the minds and hearts of those who worked here as revealed through their quirky and sometimes dark sense of humor. As we proceeded, Brogan adopted the persona of a two-bit kingpin giving me a tour of his neighborhood racket, the running joke being that he wanted it all—wanted control over all the goods, he'd say, rubbing his hands together with a mock diabolical leer on his face.

After electrical and plumbing supplies, we moved to the beer and soda warehouse. As we climbed the creaking wooden stairs to the top floor I smelled the yeasty sweetness of the beer, and swatted at a fruit fly. On the top floor, several young men and women sat behind an army-surplus desk. Nearby was an equally scruffy-looking couch of dark Naugahyde and a coffee table covered with outdated, well-thumbed magazines.

"Everything you have to have to run a community, we have here," Brogan bragged, "and we go to the store only twice a year!" He was referring to the supply ship, called the Green Wave, which arrived in Winter Quarters Bay each February, at the end of the science season. When the Green Wave pulled into McMurdo's Winter Quarters Bay in February, said Brogan, "It's a four-day party," unloading the boat and getting everything where it belongs. The entire vessel is chartered from Port Hueneme, California, carrying as much as 26 million pounds of goods, including Xerox machines and espresso makers. Aboard would be everything McMurdo needed for the winter and beyond. Everything the Green Wave brought was entered into a huge database called MAPCON, short for Material, Planning, and Control. This way, Brogan joked again, he knew *exactly* where *everything* was.

Next I saw where McMurdo stored its required two-year cache of dried and frozen food. As we entered the main warehouse we were dwarfed by eight-foot towers of boxes. It felt like walking down the canyon of a Manhattan street lined by skyscrapers, only these were bulging cardboard monoliths full of pork and beans, chili, and canned pears. This warehouse was locked, just like the booze warehouse, Brogan informed me, a special precaution taken with not just any old warehouse. I thought momentarily of the science fiction horror flick *The Thing,* where the keepers of a remote Antarctic station go berserk, haunted by a thawed-out ice mummy. I imagined similar chaos at McMurdo, the food warehouse looted by riotous, famished scientists and workers going after the cookies and canned peanuts.

"We have one thousand people a day in the summer in McMurdo," Brogan said, as if to explain the gargantuan amounts of food. "At four meals a day—that's counting midrats (the midnight meal)— that's a lot of food." He went on, chuckling, "There's an old Antarctic theory that you bring way more food than you could possibly need because you might get stuck—for a few years." Clearly, someone was planning well, although, he confided, planners are suggesting that McMurdo cut back its stored supplies to enough to last eighteen months, rather than the previously required two years. Storage space is a problem, but so is the problem of old food. He held up a bottle of ketchup—Exhibit A—dated 1987, more than a decade past its prime. A McMurdo friend told me that one year for the winter-over art show, in which winter-over residents display jewelry, woodworking, and paper crafts and even sell tapes of their own folk music, she made a collage of labels from the cans and boxes of food she'd cooked with as a chef in the McMurdo galley during the season. A significant number of the pieces of her collage revealed that the food had been dated for use circa 1960–1970—twenty to thirty years past due.

Because fresh food is expensive to transport from New Zealand to Antarctica, much of what's eaten at McMurdo is dried, canned, or frozen. In the winter, this is supplemented by small amounts of greens from McMurdo's hydroponic greenhouse—enough for a salad a week for each of the 150 or so winter-overs. In the summer, the period called "main body," which starts at the beginning of October and lasts until late January, up to 4,700 pounds of fresh food arrives each week. That averages 4.7 pounds per person, which equals two cups of yogurt, a handful of grapes, a banana and an apple, a few kiwifruits, some fresh carrots, onions and garlic mixed in with the regular food, and maybe some fresh milk if you're lucky.

Later Brogan and I tour the frozen food warehouse, a small, cool, dim building stacked floor to ceiling with grim cardboard boxes the size of washing machines. A friend scoots by on a pallet loader, the machine beeping as he heads into the dark reaches of the warehouse. Around us loom boxes of hamburger, chicken, shrimp, and sweet rolls, all of it somehow disconcerting and inhuman, like a barn full of hay or a silo full of corn.

In the carpentry shop, a cold pole shed that smelled of cut wood and paint, ear-splitting rock music was playing. A Grateful Dead skull was painted on the wall near the Departure Dartboard. Like a regular dartboard, it was divided into sections like a pie, each section labeled with one of the following: "Bumped for DV (Distinguished Visitor). Bad weather. No flight out. Planes broken down. Bumped for rock boxes. Bumped. Headwinds. Planes broken down." A handful of darts was stuck in the plywood wall next to the board, and underneath was written: "If you miss the board you're wintering over."

Although the joke made over-wintering sound dreadful, over-wintering in Antarctica made everyone who did it a hero. For doing it, you got a medal—a bona fide ribbon from which dangled a medallion pressed with an image of a person bundled up in Antarctic gear. And you got your picture taken. Upstairs in the storage area of the carpentry shop were stacks of plywood backdrops that the winter-over gang posed in front of for their winter-over picture celebrating the end of the season each August. One such sign from 1992 showed Father Winter up in one corner with wild gray hair and puffy red cheeks, blowing a fierce storm down upon the tiny town of McMurdo, a collection of ragtag buildings on a muddy, dirty outcrop of land on Ross Island. The sign read "McMurdo Station Antarctica. Winterover 1992. Way off the flagged route." "The flagged route" of the sign referred to the routes marked along the ice around McMurdo with brightly colored flags, meant to indicate safe paths among crevasses and cracks. The phrase made beautiful sense to me. Most of the people one met in Antarctica had chosen to veer off the well-mapped, "flagged route" of life—taking risks of one sort or another that delivered them here, to this miraculous wilderness of ice and stone. It made me think of Frost's road not taken. This was no New England yellow wood, but wasn't the risk the same, to take a "road less traveled by," and embrace the pains and pleasures one encountered along one's way?

Here in McMurdo, way off the flagged route, all sorts of people converged: bankers, MBAs, therapists, carpenters, and professional graphic artists were all thrown into the soup together, ending up as laundry workers, bakers, directors of recreation, and cooks at remote field camps. Navy psychologists who've done research on human culture in Antarctica as an analogue to Mars or space stations, call this phenomenon "lack of status identification." As my friend Charlotte Potter crudely put it, "We don't have a fucking clue who anyone is down here." At McMurdo, you forfeited whatever former status you had in your life "off the ice," and started again from the bottom, building your social infrastructure and identity based on something new. Your old self virtually disappeared, or became unimportant. Relationships were reduced to the most basic of levels—what *kind of a person* were you? Were you kind, how did you handle stress, and perhaps most important, did you have a sense of humor?

Humor seemed to be a common glue at McMurdo. It was important to make fun, and just about everything one did at McMurdo, indeed, everything *about* McMurdo, everything about human beings in Antarctica, seemed good enough fodder for a joke. Antarctica is a place of extremes, and extremes are what jokes are made of. There's something deeply incongruous about the whole of the human enterprise in Antarctica, about trying to maintain not just life, but sophisticated scientific inquiry, a complex bureaucracy, and humane cultural affairs and social relations in such a brutal, rudimentary place. If one took oneself and the endeavor too seriously, swallowed it whole, without the sweetening influence of humor, what would be left if you failed?

Besides the Departure Dartboard, other jokes about not being able to leave Antarctica when you wanted to abounded. I spotted this ridiculously complex formula for calculating your leave date taped to the side of a filing cabinet as Brogan led me through yet another dusty warehouse: How To Calculate Your Actual Redeployment Date: $D_1$ = first redeployment date, $D_2$ = second redeployment date, $R_d$ = actual redeployment date, X = number of times you've told your supervisor what a nice person he or she is, $W_1$ = when you'd most like to leave (of little significance), $W_2$ = why you'd most like to leave (of little significance), $W_3$ = what type of aircraft you'd most like to be on, S = sum of your social security number (example: 321-54-8778=3+2+1+5+4+8+7+7+8), E = expectation factor (x 10 to the 11th power if your mind has already left Antarctica), Pb = Place of birth, Sp = South Pole in relation to Place of Birth. The actual equation was never supplied.

In the Crary Research Lab, where Brogan took me to survey the rooms full of beakers, pipettes, and other sundry scientific supplies, I encountered, not for the first time, evidence of the macabre side of the Antarctic funny bone. In the animal room, all cool and full of the sounds of hisses and bubbles, there hung a sign above a tank full of sea spiders, sea cucumbers, sea stars, anemones, urchins, and other creepy-looking creatures that read: "Antarctic Petting Zoo. Feel free to pick up, fondle, kiss, cuddle, etc." While this seemed relatively harmless—the most one might get would be a slimy kiss or a mild sting—another joke in the lab involved a tank of Antarctic cod, some as big as Labrador retrievers. Newcomers, or "fingees" (Fucking New Guys), were sometimes encouraged to visit the cod, and even to hop in the tanks with them. In reality, the cod were aggressive and could rise out of the water to investigate anything that looked like potential food, including a face, a camera, or a hand.

What's funny about telling someone to stick their hand into a tank of flesh-eating fish? It's all in the delicate power play between who's been around and who hasn't, who knows the ropes and who doesn't, who's earned their Antarctic spurs and who hasn't.

Not all Antarctic humor was as prankish; some had a deeply political bent as well, sometimes offering grim predictions of the future of human activities in this frozen land. On my visit to the weather station at Arrival Heights, a hill above McMurdo so named because it was where one went to see ships arrive in Winter Quarters Bay, there was a cartoon pasted to the edge of a filing cabinet that was titled "After the treaty expires" or "Last night I had the strangest nightmare." The cartoon referred to the Antarctic Treaty, signed originally by twelve member nations in 1959, protecting Antarctica from the pillage of individual nations and preserving it as a domain for scientific research. The number of treaty nations has grown to forty-four. Nevertheless, the fate of the continent, which some think may hold mineral resources, is in some doubt. The cartoon showed the area now occupied by McMurdo Station covered with the likes of the Arrival Heights Mall, a Sears, a cinema, the Arrival Heights Castle Rock Resort, a Taco Bell, Scott's Discovery hut turned into a Pizza Hut, the National Science Foundation, Inc., skyscraper, a ferris wheel, a freeway, a space needle, smoke stacks, a "Visit Antarctica Land" theme park, the Acey Deucy Disco, and the McMurdo Penguin Preserve, with four bewildered penguins in a cage.

As I toured McMurdo with Brogan, I couldn't help but think of a similar tour I'd taken of the South Pole station. The first U.S. station at the South Pole was built in 1957, during the International Geophysical Year, when scientists from sixty-seven countries converged on Antarctica, making it their prime focus of study. That year the first Amundsen-Scott South Pole station was built on the surface of the ice. It is now buried by at least fifty feet of ice and snow, accessible only through a secret hole. The old base was finally abandoned in 1975, when the New Pole, the one under the shiny geodesic dome, the one I toured, was ready for habitation.

The collapsing rooms and passageways of Old Pole have been the source of many an eerie story from travelers who've illegally ventured there to see that it was like a frozen ghost town: plates of half-eaten dinner still on the tables; packages strewn open among other litter, including playing cards labeled Operation Deep Freeze; photographs of women; boxes of meat; frozen piles of human excrement; plastic flowers; and, one writer recorded, thousands of dollars worth of salvageable equipment—all scattered about, just as in the other much older huts I'd visited, as if the men living there had left in wild abandonment.

The fate of the first South Pole station repeats itself in this New Pole I'd been escorted around, for the New Pole is now nearly a second Old Pole itself. Plans existed, in 1997, to take the geodesic dome apart and perhaps transfer it to a museum. Architects' drawings for the new pole suggested all kinds of improvements in design that would prevent the next, newer station from burial, from turning into another frosty ruin some fifty years in the future.

In addition to the remains of the Old Pole, somewhere under the ice was another piece of buried Antarctic history, Roald Amundsen's Poleheim, the tent he erected upon his victorious arrival at the Pole in 1911. No one really knows where Poleheim is, no one except Skip Withrow, or at least he says he knows. Withrow, a communications engineer stationed at the Pole, had made a hobby out of calculating where he might find this very first human habitation at the farthest southern point of the globe. He'd been reading Amundsen's books and had used what he'd read, along with his skills in celestial navigation and his knowledge of the sextant, to come to what he felt was an accurate determination of where one might find the little tent.

Despite Skip's expertise and despite his desire to find Poleheim and whatever still lay inside it, chances were slim he'd be allowed to launch an expedition to recover it. It would remain, most likely, forever deeply buried in ice and snow, getting deeper with each passing year and moving slowly westward. How illustrative of the way time worked, I couldn't help but think. Previous efforts of the most profound kind—heroic acts, technological achievements, great marks in history, the makings of cultures—become buried, crushed, splintered, and scattered, and new things, new ideas, new structures, were built right on top of them, creating layers of time and human culture not unlike the layers of plants, sea creatures, and dinosaur bones archeologists uncover in their effort to write the story of our ancient past.

My last stop on the McMurdo "underbelly tour" with Don Brogan was the electronics warehouse, run by Rick Pierce. The place was lined with tightly arranged gray metal shelves spilling over with cords and cables, telephones, radios, repeaters, and computer parts.

It smelled of old dust and stale air. The sign on the door said "Psycho Hazard Area."

As we stood around in the dust and junk, Don kicked at a box as big as a coffin. He asked me to guess what was in it. I couldn't. "All of Antarctic Support Services' old office telephones, sent down to Antarctica from the home office in Denver, Colorado," he said, laughing.

"A lot of junk that's outdated gets shipped here," Rick chimed in. "McMurdo is a working museum."

"What if some day this station was abandoned," Rick asked. I couldn't help but see it, just like Scott's Discovery hut down there on the peninsula, like Shackleton's hut at Cape Royds, like the Terra Nova hut at Cape Evans, like the old South Pole station now deep under the polar ice. What if, one day, this place, too, all of McMurdo, with its dormitories, its little bowling alley, its weight room and laboratories, its pottery studio and darkroom, its laundry, its bars and fire station, its gymnasium, its medical building with its examining tables and dentist's chair, its helicopter hangar, the greenhouse, the hazardous waste shed marked with its skull and crossbones, the library with its collection of late-twentieth-century romances and detective stories, the piles and piles of tools and bolts and nuts and spools of wire and stacks of lumber, the fake palm trees and pink flamingos, its VCRs and large-screen televisions, the sheets of steel, the Heavy Shop with its front-end loaders and DC-9s, the administrators' offices in the Chalet with all their paper and files, the galley, the barber's chair, all of it, what if it all drifted over and was left to be.

"It'll never happen," Brogan said.

"Oh yes it will," Pierce said. "One day it'll be one great big icy ghost town."

I could see it clearly, then, all cold and frosty and humped over with snow. Just as the old explorers' huts have become, just as the Old Pole has become, so would McMurdo become—a scientific and cultural curiosity for people of the future. Pierce nodded his head, sure of his prediction. They would come here and loot things, scavenge a few souvenirs—a cup, a plate, an espresso machine—just as latecomers did in the now-protected huts of the early explorers. They would come and snoop around and exclaim and ponder and tell stories and make jokes and laugh about what kind of culture this must have been, with its odd customs and practices. "They'll come in here," Pierce said, his hands on his hips, head roaming up and down the shelves, eyes wide, "they'll come in here and say, *maa-aan*, look at all this junk, look at these *computers*," and Brogan and Pierce joined in a nervous, thin laugh, trying to shake off this unpleasant vision—all those hopes and dreams and efforts now buried under miles and miles of ice, made hilariously obsolete.

# AN ANTARCTIC QUINTET

I.

I'd been lying on my back, taking notes, looking up into the crystals and into that blue that still amazes me—blue so blue it was as if my eyes had broken; blue so blue it was like gas that faded away into more and more intense blue violet; beauty so expansive I couldn't contain it—I had to break to let it in. The first time I'd been in an Antarctic ice cave, months earlier, the person who took me there said that often people who go down into crevasses and into ice caves are so overcome by the blue that it makes them cry. I remembered that as I lay there on my back, taking notes, trying to draw the crystals that hung like blooms of flowers above me, trying to figure out where the blue began and where it ended.

I'd gone with nine others on this expedition to the ice caves that were part of the Erebus glacier tongue, a long spit of ancient ice spilling out onto the frozen Ross Sea from the base of Mount Erebus, Ross Island's active volcano. The caves were about an hour's drive over the ice from McMurdo Station. We'd signed up for the field trip on a sheet of paper outside the galley—it was a jaunt, free to anyone who wished to go—electricians or galley cooks who had the afternoon off, a scientist who wanted out of her lab for a few hours. As the orange truck plodded across the frozen sea, heaving over humps in the ice, we passengers packed snugly inside rolled and bumped into one another like children on a carnival ride, smiling at each other over the great roar of the truck's engine.

We went to two caves. One of them was easy to get into. You climbed a hill of snow, wriggled through a rather large opening, and slid down a slight slope into a cavern about as big as an average living room. The other cave you would miss if you didn't know it was there. You kick-stepped your way up a steep incline, then pressed your body through an opening just large enough to fit your shoulders through. Then you slid down a thin, icy tube until you landed on a shelf of thick blue ice. Next, with the aid of a rope, you climbed up and around and through a maze of tight ice walls until you reached two larger caverns, luminous with the deep turquoise and violet of glacier ice, and still as a tomb. Standing on the cold, flat floor of this second cave I felt and heard a seal's high-pitched call bounce through the ice.

It was in the first cave, though, that I lay upon my back, so intent on studying the blue around me that I was startled when I sensed that I was alone. Suddenly everyone else was gone. I reluctantly packed up my notebook and rose to leave. Once I was out of my grotto, I realized there was another person left in the blue room. It was my friend Gary Teetzel, an engineer from the Crary Lab. He and I had spent time together weeks earlier in the observation tube—an eighteeen-foot-long tube set by scientists into the cold sea near McMurdo, a tube you could climb down into and sit in and watch creatures in the dark ocean around you.

"Oh, it's you," I said to Gary, jokingly, as if, should there be anyone left in the ice cavern it would have to be *him*, and *me*. He seemed a kindred spirit—a lover of quiet and contemplation. We stood at opposite ends of this ice cavern for another ten minutes, until we heard a voice calling us to come away and board the vehicle.

As I stood, I cupped my hands around my eyes so that all I saw was the blue, and as I stared, my heart began to beat faster and my breath started to come faster and tears came to my eyes. It was that blue that made me cry. That blue. That blue violet that seems to pull you in, that makes you feel as if you're falling into it, that compels you somehow to look into it, even though it blurs your vision and confuses you. It was that blue, so enigmatic that for a moment you lose your balance in it. You don't quite know if you're in the sky, or underwater, or whether for an instant you might be in both places at once. The blue is like a frosty, vague, and endlessly deep hole in your heart. It has no edges, just color and depth. It's a color that is like some kind of yearning, some unfulfilled desire, or some constant, extreme joy. It just burns there, burns violet, burns blue.

II.

The helicopter hovered over the rugged, ice-carved mountaintop, whipping up gravel and sand. A hunched figure came running from a tent nearby, clutching a hat to its head. Out of the open helicopter door a cookstove was handed to the figure, who grabbed it and secured it under his arm. There were waves of the hand and nearly inaudible shouts of thanks, and we lifted up again, the tiny camp below us diminishing to no more than bright dots of color in the sweeping landscape of ice and stone.

I was with McMurdo technician Tracy Dahl on a morning helicopter ride up the Taylor Valley in Antarctica's Dry Valleys, the world's coldest desert—a landscape so alien it had become a testing ground for equipment the United States hoped one day to send to Mars. Dahl was to deliver the stove and other supplies to two graduate students who'd pitched their peaked, yellow canvas Scott tents on the top of a windy, gravely high plateau. The next stop was a pickup and delivery at Lake Bonney, farther up the valley, and then, finally, Dahl and I were set down outside the three uninhabited canvas jamesways that made up the Lake Fryxell camp, which Dahl was to prepare for a soon-to-be-arriving field party.

After the chores were done, Dahl and I sat beside the fuel stove in one of the jamesways and warmed our feet on its metal sides, tipped back in our chairs, drinking tea, passing the time until Dahl's helicopter arrived to take him back to McMurdo. Then I'd be on my own. I was equipped for a small expedition: radio, backpack with tent, stove, sleeping bag, extra food, and clothes. I would make my way back on foot to Lake Hoare, the field camp where I'd been staying for the week. Mine was an officially sanctioned several-hour walk. If I didn't arrive at Lake Hoare by dinnertime, there would probably be a helicopter sent from McMurdo to find me. Nevertheless, it felt like an adventure—a walk in Antarctica, a walk in the wildest place I'd ever been, a walk in what might yet be the wildest place on Earth.

Every walk, said Henry David Thoreau, that nineteenth-century American saunterer of woods and mind, is a sort of crusade—a westward going, a wildward going—a journey toward self-awareness, transformation, and the future. We should be prepared, he said, on even the shortest walk to go "in the spirit of undying adventure, never to return—prepared to send back our embalmed hearts only as relics to our desolate kingdoms." The name itself, walker, saunterer, Thoreau wrote, may have derived from the expression used to describe a person in the Middle Ages who wandered about the land, à la Sainte Terre, a pilgrim, heading toward the Holy Land. Or it might be rooted in the words sans terre, without a home, but everywhere at home.

I felt both as I set off across Lake Fryxell, my ice axe swinging like a walking stick at my side, its metal point pinging against the hard turquoise surface beneath me. The teeth of my crampons bit in as I walked: metal against ice. The blue lake ice was cut by geometric patterns of crazy white lines and rising white orbs. I felt homeless and at home in the universe, as if I, too, was a pilgrim, walking not toward, but *in* a holy land.

The flatness of the valley I was in was broken on each side by distant hills swathed in shades of brown and white, the ones to my back more mountainous and sharp, the ones facing me, softer. My way led across Lake Fryxell, so beautifully disturbed by the designs in its frozen surface, toward the edge of the Canada glacier, which spilled out of the mountains between Fryxell and Lake Hoare and which I would have to go around. I paused frequently on the walk, gazing, enthralled with patterns in the snow made by wind, so delicately and improbably shaped—like letters, like words, like whole sentences written in dark brown dust on snow. Often I would stop to simply gaze about me, down the valley where it spread out wide and met the blue and white cloud-spattered sky, behind me to see the tiny jamesways of the Fryxell camp receding, and the towering glacial wall, emanating coldness. Many times, when I paused, the glacier would crack and thunder and I would jump for fear I'd be smashed by a falling chunk of ice as big as a house, me like a fly beneath it.

Such openness I had never walked in, never traveled by foot in such intimacy with. One step at a time would take me back to Lake Hoare by evening. I savored each step, giddily feeling my strong legs hinge at the hips, feeling each stride, my lungs expanding fully, my arms swinging, my back bearing up the weight of the pack. The land here was bare bones, stripped-down, elemental, and beautiful; beautiful in the way the bleak, landless, endless ocean is beautiful to fishers; the way deserts are beautiful to Saharan nomads; beautiful in its smallness—the many-colored pebbles in my path, the ragged ice along the shore, the turquoise glass I walked upon; and beautiful in its largeness—the infinite reach of sky, the gigantic arc of the land. The land brought me back, as it did Thoreau, to my senses; back to my body, back to my self.

As I walked I pondered how the world was reached through the self, how the universal comes of the particular, the immense from the intimate. Thoreau called it "recreating self," and for it he went to the most dismal of places; he entered the darkest of woods, the swampiest of swamps; they were his sacred places, *sanctum sanctorum*—for they were the places that were truly wild. What would he have made, I wondered, of Antarctica?

The woods and meadows of nineteenth-century New England were Thoreau's wilderness. He called it a mythic land: "You may name it America, but it is not America; neither Americus Vespucius, nor Columbus, nor the rest were discoverers of it. There is a truer account of it in Mythology than in any history of America." That he walked in a mythic landscape meant to him that his journey took him into all time. Thoreau walking in his woods, me walking alone from Lake Fryxell to Lake Hoare, around the booming edge of the towering Canada glacier, was humankind, womankind, mankind walking, walking in an unknown land. You may name it Antarctica, but it is not Antarctica. All moments converge here in this place and time—all efforts at renewal, all quests for knowledge, all attempts at transformation and adventure collide here in this *solid* earth, in this *actual* world.

As I rounded the final protruding hunk of ice of the Canada glacier and came within sight of the Lake Hoare camp, I could see the tiny purple, blue, and yellow dots of the domed tents, and the glint of the sun off the small metal buildings. I pulled my radio out of the bulging deep pocket of my bibbed wind pants and called in. "W-002 calling Lake Hoare," I said, giving my Antarctic code name, the W standing for writer. The radio crackled and popped and then came the familiar voice of Bob Wharton, the head scientist at the camp. "Roger, this is Lake Hoare camp. How would you like your steak done?" It would be good to be back among them, but it had also been good to be out alone, walking in Antarctica, feeling that magical, paradoxical diminishment of self and enlargement of spirit that such a landscape brings—that feeling that one is in the presence of something that has been in existence long before you and will continue long after you, into all time; some spirit that is larger and older than the human mind, and that, in its power, comforts rather than terrifies, soothes rather than agitates.

"I believe in the forest, and in the meadow, and in the night in which corn grows . . ." wrote Thoreau. This is what he crusaded for, what he walked for—the *common sense*, the link between spirit and body, earth and self. I believed in this too—that there was a sublime power in this land that could mysteriously help a person reconnect with that subtle magnetism in wildness that would show her the way. I believed in this vast glacier-scoured landscape, this thundering ice, and in the impossible simplicity of the thin line between frozen earth and sky.

III.

Antarctica is famous for wind, wind that roars down the mountains from the polar plateau, spilling into the ocean; *katabatic* wind, fast wind, wind that carves ice into feathers and ferns; wind that carves rock into wind facts, *ventifacts*, signifiers of wind, something solid made of the workmanship of wild air.

The wind howling in around the seams in the McMurdo galley door is a sound I'll remember from Antarctica. Wind screaming in on stormy days, at a higher pitch than I could sing, sounding so much like a piece of machinery gone haywire, or an animal caught short, surprised or afraid. I'll remember the wind at the windows, knocking in a thick, padded, muffled way, so that you might imagine there was someone out there, wanting you to *open up*, *open up*, let them in. And the wind whistling down the hollow shaft of a bamboo pole, one in a line planted out there in the middle of nowhere showing the way to safety, the way home, the way around a deadly crack in the ice. The wind whistled down the shaft, as if the pole were a bamboo flute and wind was playing on it a merry, eerie tune.

I'll remember, too, the sound of the small cotton flags tied to those poles—red and green for follow me this way, black for go this way and you'll die—the flags, *slap, slap, slapping* in the wind, snapping against themselves, cracking like whips in the 100-degrees-below-zero air.

I'll remember the wind *whoop, whoop, whoop, whooping* through the electrical and telephone wires. In one spot, behind McMurdo's two bars, the winds whipped and howled and *moaned* and *moaned* and *moaned* around the buildings, into nooks and out again, eddying and swirling, dancing and buzzing through the wires overhead, playing the wires as if they were the strings of a deep bass, pushing me along, pushing me, hurrying me along so forcefully that I had to lean back into the strength of the wind to stand upright.

I'll remember the almost nothing sound of wind across the ice, smooth and moving fast, blowing from nowhere to everywhere, taking with it my breath, the snow at my feet, the fur of my parka hood, and all of my heat.

IV.

Siple Dome camp was simple and spare: a small runway, a collection of tents and canvas jamesways surrounded by mounds of snow-buried gear and supplies. Beyond that there was nothing familiar, nothing kind to human flesh or desire, only miles-thick ice and snow, only *the fresh and natural surface of the planet Earth, as it was made forever and ever.*

Thoreau's words came to me then, again, as I marveled at how *wild* the space around me was, how nobly spacious, how elemental, and how being here grounded me undeniably in my own flesh. Siple Dome, a scientific field camp on the West Antarctic Ice Sheet, was a place by all accounts in the middle of absolutely nowhere, where one could turn 360 degrees and not see the horizon alter its unwaveringly straight face; where one was surrounded by a wilderness of snow and ice stretching as far as the mind could imagine; wildness so extreme it could extinguish you in a blink, as quickly as if you were being drowned, as quickly as if you'd been set free in outer space with no oxygen.

Before the cooks, electricians, carpenters, and scientists at Siple Dome could even begin the work of setting up the field station and going about their research, they had to shovel the camp out from beneath yards and yards of snow that had buried it over the Antarctic winter. Now this unlikely village lay atop the snow and ice, looking ever so much like a nomadic encampment in a wide, icy desert, at any moment prone to being blown away, to being buried again, to being neatly erased from the face of the earth.

Kendrick Taylor, from the Desert Research Institute in Reno, Nevada, a man who studies ice, drove out with me on a sunny Sunday to a spot ten kilometers from the camp, following a line of green flags on bamboo poles that marked a safe route along the snow. When we reached the end of the flag line, we stopped our snowmobiles and Kendrick said to me, pointing into nowhere, at nothing, "Go ahead another two kilometers and turn off your machine and sit. I'll wait here."

I drove out toward a horizon like I'd never seen. I imagined that, had I kept going, I could have driven right off the edge of the planet. The only thing separating the land from the sky in this place was a thin white line and the faintest change in hue from white to pale blue. The snowy wind moved like a fog over the ground, a slinky, elegant, snaky thing, throwing off my sense of balance, blurring the edges of my vision.

I drove for two kilometers, watching the odometer as I went. Then I stopped, turned off the machine, and sat in the quiet. I looked behind me for Kendrick and saw only a dark speck in the distance, surrounded by an immensity of blankness, sky and ground inextricably fused. I got off the snowmobile and lay down in the snow. I spread out my legs and my arms as if I were making a snow angel. I could feel the hard coolness of the ice all along my back and legs. *Contact!* Here it was beneath me. Here I was upon it—Thoreau's *solid* earth! *Here was no man's garden, but the unhandseled globe.* All I heard was the sharp hiss of the wind blowing crystals of snow over me, past my ears, and across my face. All I felt was my body against matter. How comical I must have looked and how tiny; an amalgam of flesh and bone, nylon and rubber in the midst of that Titanic ice. But who would have seen? I shut my eyes and must have been lulled by the wind, hypnotized by the cold, because I was roused only when a snowmobile engine broke my reverie. It was Kendrick coming to get me. I looked down at my legs, my arms, my boots— they were covered with snow, the black of my wind pants now white. The snow had begun to conceal me, as it had buried the pallets of cargo lined up around Siple Dome camp, as it had drifted over the jamesways themselves. How easily, how effortlessly, I could have disappeared; how easily any of us could, and how inexplicably this knowledge of our smallness, of my smallness, filled me with joy.

V.

At the South Pole, I wandered out from the silver geodesic dome into the searing white light of late afternoon. It was always bright day outside at the Pole, the sun overhead, circling around and around and around this spot at the bottom of the world, hardly dipping, never setting. I wore snow goggles, my furred parka hood was cinched tight, leaving just a peephole, fur-backed gauntlets covered my hands and lower arms, a fleece neck gaiter protected my cheeks and nose from freezing. I breathed with difficulty in the thin, 10,000-foot-high air, and the gaiter over my face thickened with frost. It was the beginning of summer at the South Pole, and it was minus 75.1 degrees Fahrenheit.

When I looked to the horizon I saw only white and blue, separated by a subtle line between the ice and sky that bowed around, encircling me in the curve of the globe. I walked out from the geodesic dome toward the two most famous landmarks at the South Pole—the mirrored ball atop the red-and-white-striped barber pole ringed by flags that is the ceremonial pole, and the small, non-descript surveyor's marker that is the exact location of the geographical South Pole, the southern axis of the planet Earth. At the ceremonial pole, the flags slapped in the wind and added stunning color to the all-white landscape. The flags are those of the original nations that signed the Antarctic Treaty—a treaty that preserves Antarctica as the only continent on the globe free from national ownership, resource extraction, development, plundering, and wreck; a treaty meant to preserve the continent in perpetuity "for peaceful purposes."

A short distance away from the barber pole was the survey marker, about three feet high, a metal pole atop which sits a thick, gold-colored disk imprinted with an image of the Antarctic continent itself. Also pressed into the top of the disk are the words "Planet Earth. Geographical South Pole. 90 Degrees South. January 1, 1997." The marker is dated because the ice here shifts westward about thirty feet a year, making it necessary to replot the exact location of the pole on the first new day of each year. When I looked up and squinted into the distance, I could see a long line of such markers trailing away into the snowy flatness.

A friend had entrusted me, before I left my home in Anchorage, Alaska, with some ashes in a small glass vial. They were remains from her mother and sister. In the past she'd given such vials to others who'd gone to places such as the summit of Denali or to other ends of the earth. I said I'd find a place for her mother and sister at the bottom of the world, so I had the vial in the pocket of my red parka. I dug a small impression in the snow with the heel of my boot and, with my hands still in my ungainly mittens, fumbled the vial open and sprinkled ashes into the hole. I covered the spot and stamped it down, thinking that in weeks, months, next year, the ice would move on, taking the ashes with it, westward; one day they'd make it out to the continent's edge, fall into the sea, melt, be taken up by the circumpolar currents and make their way around the globe. Then they would be everywhere. I bowed toward the marker, toward the center, and I said a prayer—for my friend who'd lost her mother and sister, one to a heart attack and one to suicide; for me, whose sister also took her own life; for all of us, for all of our grief, for all of our delicate, human suffering.

Afterward, in the dull, stinging cold, I stared for a time at the words on the survey marker. "Planet Earth. Geographical South Pole." The geographical South Pole. The other end of the world from the place I lived. Everywhere I looked from here, from this exact spot, was north. If I walked around this spot, I'd be walking around the world, through all the time zones, from one day to the next, into the future, through the past and out again. . . . I did it. I put my mittened hand on the head of the marker, feeling the impression of the continent through the leather and lining, and I walked around it. I walked around and around and around the world, my steps creaking in the dry hard snow. I'd never felt so riveted in place, so exactly located, so precisely in one spot, and everywhere at once.

# NACREOUS CLOUDS

Ruth walked briskly into McMurdo's Crary Lab, making her way down the tiled corridors in her scuffed work boots and blue jeans, her pockets full of pliers and wire strippers, a pair of leather gloves hanging out the back of her pants, passing by the doors of others who called out to her cheerfully, happy to see her. But she didn't stop to talk to anyone else; she came directly to *my* door. She said hello, and then she said she wanted to show me something beautiful. My breath caught, and for a moment I was confused. *What?* She explained that she and her friend Russell Bixby, a McMurdo computer technician, were headed up to Arrival Heights, a weather station perched on the hills above McMurdo, to see the nacreous clouds forming right now, this minute, in the wide Antarctic sky, and I *must come!*

I had work to do, I said, apologizing, and at the same time feeling thrilled at the special invitation. *No, you must come!* she insisted. The prospect of going out into the cold deterred me. I would have to turn off my computer, don my parka, my wind pants, my boots, my hat, my fleece neck gaiter, my mittens. It would be a *lot* of trouble. At the moment I was warm and nicely situated. I had, earlier that morning, collected some information about how refrigeration works in Antarctica, thinking it might make an interesting story— an interview with the engineer in charge of keeping things cold in the coldest place on earth.

This is the kind of writing I felt obligated to do in Antarctica—writing about facts and lives other than my own; writing that approached Antarctica objectively, as a journalist might, with a clear plan. But the truth of it was, I was somewhat at a loss. I was beginning to sense that the preconceived ideas I'd come to Antarctica with, the ideas about what stories I might find and tell, didn't fit or feel quite right. I'd written anxiously to a writing mentor, telling her that I felt I needed to make a show of keeping busy here or I'd look like the slacker everyone knows writers to be, while, in fact, what I really wanted to do was wander around and simply look at things, or better yet, sit still and stare at things, or listen without asking questions. She responded by telling me that being "lazy" was a writer's job—it was only in this open state that a writer would truly see.

It was hard advice to follow. I told Ruth I needed to finish the story I was working on and turned tentatively back to my computer screen. She shrugged, raising her dark eyebrows as if to say, *don't blame me later for your regrets. Come now and I'll show you something you've never seen! Stay here and you'll miss your chance. It'll be gone and you'll always wonder what might have been.* In the end, I was seduced by her enthusiasm and by my own curiosity; seduced, too, by the fact that she'd come to *my* door. What were they, these nacreous clouds that had everyone, including Ruth, so excited, and what did it mean that she wanted to share them with *me*?

We squished into the front seat of her battered pickup truck and crunched over the gravelly road, growling up the hill. I was conscious of Ruth's shoulder and thigh against mine on one side, and

Russell's bigger, heavier body on the other. There was a buzz of energy among the three of us. Russell chattered excitedly. *Nacreous*, he explained, came from *nacre*, meaning mother-of-pearl—a name that attempted to describe the nearly indescribable beauty of the clouds that shine on Antarctica only for a brief week or so each year, glinting like the silvery insides of ocean shells. The clouds start forming during the Antarctic winter and gradually disappear as the light returns. The clouds had begun gathering that afternoon, and the whole of McMurdo was on watch. People had hauled out their photographic equipment and walked or driven like us to the top of Arrival Heights to await the spectacle, spreading out their tripods along the ridge.

What I saw, standing on the hill looking out over the sea ice toward the horizon, close to Ruth, our parka fabric touching, were clouds spread thin and long, delicate and intricate, in iridescent blues, greens, yellows, and reds. It was, as the name so aptly suggests, like the inside of a monstrous oyster, an oyster whose shell we were all standing in, Lilliputian, staring upward, mouths agape. The darkening evening sky was full of wisps of colored clouds, lit brilliantly from below by a setting sun. "Floating rainbows," someone standing with us on the ridge called them. We were dumbstruck, all of us.

They're so otherworldly, these clouds, that photographs don't do them justice, don't urge their beauty into full expression. The best representations I've seen of them are in watercolors by Edward Wilson, that enigmatic scientist-artist who was part of both of Robert Falcon Scott's Antarctic expeditions. Wilson used electric blues, lime greens, crimsons, violets, and fluorescent oranges to give life to his nacreous clouds, in the shapes of wild serpents snaking across the sky. In 1903 he wrote in his journal of the clouds:

> In the North at noon there was a splendid sunrise with a heavy bank
> of cloud arranged for all the world like wavy hair, and wherever the
> sunlight caught those waves and curls it was broken into the most
> delicate opal mother-o'-pearl tints; all colors of the rainbow, pale rose,

pure lilac, emerald green, lemon yellow, and fiery red—blending but with no apparent arrangement. . . . If a dozen rainbows were broken up and scattered in wavy ribands and flecks of curl and fleecy forms to float against a background of dull gray, it would be something like the beautiful appearance of this cloud coloring.

In his effort to bring these amazing clouds to words, to get the colors right, Wilson even resorted to chemistry, saying that the clouds made him think of a "vacuum tube with a current sparkling through it, or perhaps the color is more exactly what you get with an incandescent barium."

A scientist standing next to me sighed, shook his head, and said aloud, "Sad clouds." I asked him what he meant. Although the clouds were strikingly beautiful, he said, as beautiful as anything in the natural world that had ever moved man or woman to tears, to ecstasy, they were also agents of destruction. They were the platforms upon which the destruction of the earth's ozone layer was taking place. Every year the ozone hole opens over the Antarctic, getting bigger and bigger until the end of October, when it starts healing naturally, as the air over Antarctica mixes with more ozone-rich air from mid-latitudes. By December, there is almost no noticeable ozone hole over the Antarctic. But, even though the hole heals itself each season, there is still an overall global loss of ozone each year, a loss that is expected to intensify in the next several decades.

The ozone layer is what shields Earth from ultraviolet light. Under ideal circumstances, when ultraviolet light hits the ozone layer, the ozone layer absorbs it, protecting the planet from its harmful rays. Without the ozone layer there is little to stop the high frequency, low wavelength UV light from reaching Earth—causing skin cancer, dramatic global climate changes, and possibly other damage to the foundation of our material being—our very DNA. As we watched the clouds waver and curl, their colors folding and fading, we were watching the very chemical reactions that eat holes in the earth's protective cloak.

Such beauty, and such destruction. The forces were almost impossible to reconcile, yet here they existed, together, in this sublime moment. Some fire was kindling in me as well. I burned with something. It felt unlikely and shy, here in this rough, beautiful, awful place. It was a kind of excitement that was like, for lack of any better word, *love*, but no kind I'd ever felt before—not the kind you feel for a person, but the kind you might feel for something bigger than the human. Like Henry David Thoreau, America's ecstatic, priestly nature lover, on his journey up Mount Ktaadn, I, too, was in a place so hard and vast that I felt spellbound with awe. Talk about hard matter in its home! Standing atop Arrival Heights, under the light of those incandescent clouds, I felt as Thoreau must have when he was moved to cry out: "This was that Earth of which we have heard, made out of Chaos and Old Night. . . . Talk of mysteries! Think of our life in nature,—daily to be shown matter, to come in contact with it,—rocks, trees, wind on our cheeks! the *solid* earth! the *actual* world! the *common* sense!"

If I hadn't gone with Ruth, I might never have experienced this sublimity at all. Whatever had made me want to stay inside at my computer? Whatever had made me consider not accepting her invitation? Was it lethargy? Lack of imagination? Or was it my old friend, fear?

Five years before traveling to Antarctica, I'd left my marriage, having accepted finally that I wasn't meant, after all, to be with men. Coming out as a lesbian was for me a great awakening—a coming into my body and into a new vision of my self that was so powerful it felt like an explosion, a violent and joyous rebirth. I'd ridden the wave of that momentous change, discovering depths to my sexual desire I'd never imagined, discovering vital connections between who I was, what I thought, what I felt, and the real flesh and bone of my body. It had been a dizzy time of discovery and boldness. I exercised a recklessness I'd never permitted myself as a teenager.

I was introduced to lesbian culture through movies and books, and, without shame for the first time in my life, allowed myself to joyfully satisfy the desires those fictions lit in me. I went to bars, where, dressed in tight black jeans and thin white singlets, I smoked, drank beer, and danced, with women! I learned how to two-step. I shaved my head. I fell deeply and passionately in love for the very first time in my life, and I had my heart broken. All of this in so few years—the whole of my sexual awakening zippered up into this impossibly brief span of time. Then I was "out"; out in the world as a lesbian, out on my own as a professional writer and teacher, no longer part of the sweet cocoon of old and new friends I'd woven around myself in graduate school, but a new person in a new land, trying to find my way.

I'd thought lesbian life would be easy, that love would come smoothly, that the whole of my living from the moment I declared my new self would be gravy. The reality was that real love, regardless of who it's with, is at once the most magical and the most difficult of undertakings. The great struggle of love is to reach a balance between what we want, what we imagine we deserve, what is offered to us, and what we accept. I hadn't yet reached that place of balance.

My most recent relationship had run aground on a rocky spot just months after it started. I'd been telling my lover that all I wanted in life was to be with someone who adored me. "You'll never find that; that's impossible," she said. "You're too old for that to happen now." It was as if she'd said "Abandon ship. All hope is lost." I believed her. My expectations were too high. I didn't really want to be adored, or to adore someone in return. That kind of love didn't really exist, and besides, I told myself, I probably didn't deserve it anyway.

Ruth's invitation to gaze upon those clouds was an opening, an opportunity. *I want to show you something beautiful*, she'd said, and my heart had leapt. The part of me that wanted to stay safely in front of my computer with my already-imagined stories of Antarctica was a part of me that wanted to follow a well-trodden path. To open up to experience, instead of plotting everything out, including the stories that Antarctica might offer, was opening a window to the unknown, and, though I fancied myself an adventurer, I was timid in the face of a real opportunity to see what might be out there. What was out there could be anything, including love. The first signs are subtle, after all. *You must come*, she'd said. Part of me didn't want to go through all that business of opening my heart to someone new. Ruth would be leaving McMurdo soon, having completed fourteen months on the ice. No one was allowed to stay much longer than that before being sent away to rejuvenate themselves in some different clime. What would be the use of falling in love with someone who was about to fly away to who knows where?

But I'd taken the first step, and one thing led to another. I was on the hill above McMurdo, with Ruth and Russell, with half of McMurdo, watching the clouds that shone and glimmered like pearl, like fire, like incandescent potassium, like light through the petal of a rose; clouds so shockingly beautiful that their glory was as hard and bright as their destructive portent.

The last time they'd gazed, awestruck, at the shimmering beauty of such clouds, Russell was saying, "The sea was orange and peach, the mist was blue, like a navy blue fog. Over there the black mountain was poking out above the navy blue sky and the clouds made serpentine patterns. The sky was a deep midnight blue. Against it the clouds were like a stained-glass window into heaven." Ruth, who'd wanted to bring me here to see this spectacular vision, turned, smiling, and asked me, "Aren't you glad now that you came with me?" *Oh yes*, I said. I was.

# PAINTING WITH LIGHT

Any human-built thing comes as a shock in Antarctica; any piece of matter that isn't dirt or snow or ice leaps alarmingly forward. But when we first approached the Cape Evans hut from the ice, it seemed instead to fold into the landscape, into the dirt and ice and snow around it, into the gentle hills still scattered with broken wooden boxes, tools, and, I heard tell of but didn't see, the mummified carcass of a sled dog, one of an original thirty-four, still chained to the ground. The whole thing seemed like wreckage; inconsequential in a way—a weathered shack, partly drifted over, a crooked ladder leaning under a side roof; some part of history that was sinking back into the elements from which it had come, being reabsorbed by the earth.

I was on adventure with Ruth again, this time with our friend Tom Learned and scientist Donal Manahan. Manahan, also a historian of Antarctica, had enlisted Learned to help him recreate a series of famous photographs taken in Robert Falcon Scott's Cape

Evans hut by Scott's expedition photographer Herbert Ponting, who was appointed "camera artist" to the Terra Nova expedition, thereby becoming one of the first professional photographers to go to Antarctica. This was the hut that served as the launch point for Scott's journey to the pole in 1911–12. It was also the base from which Scott's chief scientist, Edward Wilson, set out for Cape Crozier in search of emperor penguins, a journey that Apsley Cherry-Garrard later wrote about in *The Worst Journey in the World*.

Manahan would pose with me and Ruth, the three of us representing members of that fateful Cape Crozier expedition: I was Cherry-Garrard, "the writer"; Ruth was Henry "Birdie" Bowers, aka Mr. Fix-it; and Manahan was Wilson. These were the three who took off across the ice in the dead of winter for the penguin colony, in the name of science, and nearly died, coming back skeletons of themselves, hardly recognizable. Manahan also posed as Ponting, standing beside his 6 x 8 darkroom, in which he worked and slept— the room still scattered with remnants of his trade. He stood, again as Wilson, next to the scientific table, a stark, white Antarctic sun coming in a small window, beating down through the dust motes, setting test tubes, glass pipettes, metal stands and clamps, beakers and scattered papers aglow.

In addition to being Scott's chief scientist, Wilson was an artist, working chiefly in watercolors and pastels. He did most of his watercolor painting in a corner in the Cape Evans hut. Cherry-Garrard writes that Wilson returned to the hut regularly with "a note-book filled with such sketches of outlines and colours: of sunsets behind the Western Mountains: of lights reflected in the freezing sea or in the glass houses of the ice foot: of the steam clouds on Erebus by day and of the Aurora Australis by night."

Wilson's works, many of which are archived at the Scott Polar Research Institute in Cambridge, England, are filled with and focused on light. He drew ice, penguins, the sea, birds, auroral displays, men at work, hoosh mugs and spoons, his companions in states of labor and repose, ponies, air, storms, mountain ranges, and camp scenes. He drew and painted some of the same scenes over and over, particularly icebergs, the Barrier edge, Mount Erebus, changing sky and clouds over the Transantarctic Mountains and Winter Quarters Bay—recording the glorious shifts in color and light.

In his subtle sketch of Castle Rock, on Ross Island near Discovery Point, Wilson's browns, blues, and whites are so clear that the rocks come lifting off the paper, giving the picture a breathtaking and unexpected depth. The sky behind the blunt-topped monolith is a forever-reaching yellow and peach, orange and gold, fading upward into lavender and deep blue. In his numerous versions of the Barrier edge, Wilson presents the 100-foot-high continental ice edge sometimes in stark, high light, sometimes in gray, shaded light. Sometimes the Barrier ice is alive with turquoise and blue. Some of his pictures show the thin line of turquoise that runs along the edge of the ice and water, some explore a certain unearthly lavender in the cracks, some record a faint reflection of berg in the water.

Several of Wilson's pictures depict nearly identical perspectives of Winter Quarters Bay from near the base of Observation Hill, looking generally north, with the low rounded hills of Hut Point and the 1902 expedition's ship, *Discovery*, silhouetted darkly in the background. The pictures differ substantially only in levels and intensities of light. One can imagine Wilson sitting in the same rocky, icy spot, wearing a thick parka and boots, his sketch pad in his lap, the little pouch in which he carried it beside him, with the pencils tied on so they wouldn't be blown out of his hands. There he sat, sketching in shapes and forms and noting the colors that he would later lay in: "blue and pink" in an upper sky, followed by "blue and pink and green," "green and yellow and orange," "orange, orange, black/purple," "violet and dark purple." I can see him, sitting there, at all times of day, enduring what he mockingly called the "joys" of painting in the Antarctic:

> My eyes have been in a sorry state all day from sketching with
> sunglare, streaming with water and very painful from time to time.

Sketching in the Antarctic is not all joy, for apart from the fact that your fingers are all thumbs, and are soon so cold that you don't know what or where they are, 'til they warm up again in the tent (then you know all about it!); apart from this you get colder and colder all over, and you have to sketch when your eyes stop running, one eye at a time, through a narrow slit in the snow goggles. No one knows till they have tried it how jolly comfortable it is.

Inside the Cape Evans hut the air was still and cold and thick with dark. It was utterly black but for the light coming in the one window near the science bench. We all four peered around, walking carefully, on tiptoe, whispering, our hands out in front of us for protection. The hut itself was fifty by twenty-five feet. It was eight feet high at the eaves, and sixteen feet at the center of the ceiling. Originally it was separated into two sections by a wall of provisions, one section reserved for the sixteen officers and scientists, and one section for the nine seamen. One long wooden table occupied the center. Upon it sat an oil lamp, a china vase, and a covered enamel dish. Against the walls were bunk beds—Manahan could identify the specific beds of individual men—piled with blankets and caribou hides; mittens hung from nails on the walls. There were also personal effects: pictures, books, and the small important things one might carry in one's pockets. The back of the hut held Ponting's darkroom, the science area, and off to the side, shielded by thin walls, Scott's study area and bed, laid still with one of the expedition's thick caribou hide sleeping bags. On the table in Scott's cubbyhole lay a frozen emperor penguin, with its scaly webbed feet and sleek, creamy, yellow chest.

The front of the hut was taken up on one side by the kitchen—a massive stove, tin cups, silverware, plates, and stacks of food, some of it rearranged and cataloged by members of the Antarctic Heritage Trust, but much of it just as it was left in 1912: oatmeal and salt, Scotch kale, Indian relish, and candles. The label on the candles read: "Belmont Stearine Candles. Made Expressly for Hot Climates by Prices' Patent Candle Company," and was illustrated with an elaborate etching of a palm tree beneath which sat dark-skinned people in robes stirring a pot over a fire. These were candles made to be burned in India or other hotter realms of Britain's empire, not in the coldest place on earth. Indeed, the whole place felt like a meeting point for so many improbably different worlds, ideas, times, and desires. One chapter in the Reader's Digest coffee table volume on Antarctica, a chapter titled "Winter at Cape Evans," reports that the hut became "the southernmost outpost of the Empire as well as the wardroom and mess deck of a Royal Navy vessel. And the Edwardian social and naval attitudes, the club-like atmosphere, brought into the hut along with the Nellie Melba records and the volumes of Browning and Tennyson, hint at the reasons Scott's final expedition was such a mixture of real achievement, heroic endurance and eventual tragedy."

Across from the kitchen was an area that looked like it might have been for lounging. There lay a checkerboard and several books. One was titled *Tit Bits Vol. XLIX September 23rd, 1905 to March 17th, 1906*, a compendium of interesting facts. The table of contents included: Money, novel schemes for raising. Kisses, feast of. Kisses, some famous. Garden, world's highest. Hats, singular for eccentric heads. Hobbies, blind people's queer. Honeymooning, near the North Pole. Husbands who desert their wives. Plum pudding, for thirteen. Also on the table was a dusty copy of the *Essays of Sir Francis Bacon,* including "Of Followers and Friends," "Of Truth," "Of Death," "Of Boldness."

During the long winter in this hut the men had prepared for their polar journey, sewing up the proper footwear and planning the sledging rations. They read and sang to one another, and lectured to one another about science and art, a tradition that continues at McMurdo with the Sunday Science Lecture. I was told this was a time when Scott suffered from what is now known as seasonal affective disorder. It was all evident in his journal, I was told. And later, when I read the journal more carefully, this was something I thought I, too, could see—something interior, something small and personal, something that all the heroic accounts would try to erase, not just with Scott, but with most of the explorers—something intimate, some doubt, some sadness, some life drama that would not make its way forward into the final, official account, but was nevertheless there, informing the final outcome.

Why are these indications of human frailty erased, flooded over with official stories of high purpose? I suppose one is apt, always, to put some things in and leave some things out, but why has the personal so long been defined as somehow gossipy or small, beyond or below the reach of proper recording? But then, would we have wanted to know which one of them, in this hut, pined after what sweetheart, whether any of these men had fallen in love with one another, what they did to satisfy their sexual desires, who had doubts, who hated whom? *I* would have wanted to know. And why not? Why obscure the intimate? Why shorten the story of the glorious complexity and depth of the human in order to make a neater, grander tale?

This pondering over the importance of the personal led me to reflect on my own story, the story of my falling in love with Ruth. I knew then that I would write about her. My falling in love with her was inextricably bound up with my being in Antarctica—I couldn't separate these experiences, nor make true sense of them in isolation. I realized that, like many who'd written about Antarctica before me, I could choose to tell some other tale of heartiness and wonder, resigning the personal to the sidelines, or to a locked diary. But to leave Ruth out of the stories I would later tell would be a lie. The story of my opening to her was also the story of my opening to myself, and to the land.

We entered enthusiastically into an intimate dance, sharing with one another the stories of our previous lives. Like me, Ruth had been married for a short time. Like me, she loved the woods as a child, stalking through the trees on tiptoe, like the true woods creature she knew herself to be, and building forts that she protected from her marauding brothers with ready piles of stones. Unlike my family, hers was poor. Her father was a stevedore in Boston, then a mail carrier, her mother a full-time homemaker with ten children and a baking business on the side.

My family, I told her, was small, middle-class, from the suburbs, with a professor for a father and a mother who made art. Ruth had been partners for eight years with a woman who brought her coffee in bed, every morning, and with whom she shared a painting business. She'd loved baseball, was better at it than all of the boys, played whole games by herself with a mitt and a ball, against the garage door, yelling out the plays.

I'd been a Girl Scout, I told her. I read a lot of books. We'd traveled a lot—to Panama, Mexico, Australia—for my father's scientific work studying turtles. My mother liked to collect weeds and spray paint them gold. Ruth's father made afghans and kites and old-fashioned donuts. He loved to tinker. He had a horrible temper and once smashed all the dining room chairs. He was drawn to new things and would bring home people he met on his mail route, especially people who were different from him. He wanted to go to Alaska and Australia, but he died too soon. I went to graduate school in English, I told her, but really, I'd always wanted to be either a pirate or a private detective.

Falling in love—with the land, or with a person, in a dance that made it hard to sort out which one prepared the heart for the loving embrace of the other, the land for the woman, the woman for the land—this was part of the beauty and burden of Antarctica. I'd heard it from scientists who'd been to the ice year after year: people fall in love in Antarctica. Rice University marine scientist Rob Dunbar, whom I met aboard the icebreaker the *Nathaniel B. Palmer*, had said it: "It's easy for people to fall in love down here." Scientist Bob Wharton, whom I'd met at Lake Hoare in the Dry Valleys, had said it, too, as if it was one of the mysteries of this place yet to be plumbed, something inexplicable that science had yet to unriddle: "Lots of people fall in love in Antarctica." Like the two young graduate students, for instance, who were lollygagging behind Wharton and me as we walked along the edge of Lake Hoare on an after-dinner hike. We waited for them, watched them talking to one another, walking so close that their ice axes knocked together and their shoulders bumped. Wharton winked at me knowingly and we went on.

Perhaps the continent contributes to creating a sense of openness, a feeling of vulnerability, a sense that one is *so insignificant* in the big scheme of things that love then becomes more important rather than less; one sees, as Thoreau wrote, "our own limits transgressed," and so one goes toward the unknowable center, where the heart is.

Everyone could plainly see that Ruth and I were in love. The signs are universal, after all. We found ways to sit next to one another, to be where the other was, on purpose and by accident. We smiled openly and constantly in one another's presence. We danced together in McMurdo's smoky bar, me leading Ruth in the two-step. We had a friend take a picture of us, spinning around under the Budweiser sign to Cheryl Wheeler's country song "Silver Lining." We prowled around McMurdo at night, giggling and bumping up against one another, Ruth teaching me to shoot baskets in the deserted gym, entering even the quiet Chapel, where we stood before the stained glass window of the penguin and kissed. We lay next to one another on the floor of her room. We told each other stories. I drew her pictures. She sang me songs. She gave me candy bars and made me sculptures out of electrical wire. We were drawing ourselves together in the way that seems effortless and inevitable when one is first in love. Whether or not either one of us was ready, whether or not we knew the way or were just stumbling forward into the darkness, into something new that we would create together, we had begun it.

Ruth and I were painting with light. In the pitch dark of the Cape Evans hut, she would hold the shutter of her camera open while I shone the flashlight and swept it with easy broad strokes over our subject—a wall of canned foods, a shelf of blue and amber-colored bottles that once held medicines, the frozen emperor penguin on Scott's table, a box of penguin eggs. It was funny how the painting with light worked. Tom Learned showed us how to do it. You set the camera on a tripod in a corner in the dark, opened the shutter wide, and hoped for the best. The open eye of the camera remembered and recorded each illuminating sweep of the flashlight, bringing to light these artifacts and lives that lived steeped in quiet darkness.

We moved out to the stables, where the Siberian ponies Scott had brought with him from Europe had been kept. Ponting had taken film footage of Scott's men playing with the ponies on the snow; the ponies frolicked, the men laughed, as if they'd all been in some snowy farmyard in England. The ponies, like the dogs, all ended up dead, but the stables still smelled of hay, still smelled, after all the years, of pony. I reached a hand up to wipe away a spider web, as one would in a barn, then realized that of course there would be none there.

Ruth posed the camera, held open the shutter, and I brushed the flashlight over the wooden stalls, over the names of the ponies on signs nailed to the frosted walls—Rani, Pujaree, Gulab, Abdullah, Begum, Khan Sahib. I could imagine their breath, steaming clouds of it coming from their soft nostrils. I swept the flashlight over boxes of leather pony snowshoes, disks laced like human snowshoes with rawhide webbing, meant to help the ponies stay afloat in the snow. There was a canvas feed bag, with the litter of oats still inside it. These pictures would come out, later, a rich gold, streaked with lines of deeper and lighter gold where my flashlight had passed more than once, or failed to pass, failing to fully illuminate some detail.

That same gold color would light up the picture of Ruth that I took as she stood in the entryway to Scott's hut, the same light that made her firm, smooth, tanned face shine, rimed by her gigantic fur-ruffed parka hood, her smile wide and lovely. The extreme deep yellow of the Antarctic evening made it seem that the whole of her, the whole of the hut that had been so gray and dark when we arrived, the whole of the icy wall of the Barne Glacier that spread out beyond Cape Evans, was gilded, coated in golden light.

The most subtle and some say the most beautiful light in Antarctica occurs during just this time, the time when we four were touring Scott's hut at Cape Evans, during the Antarctic spring, the period starting in mid-August, just after the Antarctic winter, when the sun begins again to rise and set. This is the time just after the long-absent sun has begun to peek tentatively up above the horizon, just high enough to send a few rays of brilliant warm yellow into the still dark sky.

The sun will rise and set, then, from August through October, making its way through the motions most of us find predictable and comforting: dawn, day, dusk, dark. Then comes the harsh light of Antarctica's summer. From October until February the Antarctic sun never sets. There is eternal day, made blindingly bright by the white snow and ice that are Antarctica. The continent itself is so bright that astronauts looking down upon Earth from outer space have called Antarctica a white lantern shining at the bottom of the globe.

The eternal day of the Antarctic summer begins to ebb in mid-February, when the sun quits its high-in-the-sky circling and begins again to rise and set, following that familiar pattern that most of our bodily clocks are attuned to, creating day and night, morning and evening. Finally, total darkness settles in at the end of April. During the Antarctic winter the only light comes from cold bright stars and the aurora australis, which scatters the sky with bands of dancing light.

It is the low angle of the Antarctic sun that makes the colors during springtime so vivid, so paintable, so photographable. Each morning and evening the mountains, the sea ice, towering Mount Erebus, the edges of the glaciers, the old wooden explorers' huts, and the newer prefabricated metal buildings of the usually dingy town of McMurdo glowed peach and pink, nearly neon, buttery yellow, lavender, jade, and indigo. The first image I'd ever seen of this light was in a watercolor painted by Wilson in the early 1900s, of a steaming Mount Erebus in colors of such pale delicacy the work seemed forced. The colors seemed improbable in a natural setting—colors one would never associate with a landscape normally dressed in hues of black, white, gray, and brown. But Wilson's painting was enchanting, and true—the light did indeed transfigure the landscape and everything upon it, as if by sorcery.

When I first arrived in McMurdo, I could look out across the sea ice at the Transantarctic Mountains and see the peaks revealed as simple, dark, one-dimensional shapes in the distance, against skies that were lit up like fire, or washed in cool blues and pinks. Once when I was out exploring ice caves near the Erebus glacier tongue as evening came on, I watched as the entire towering edge of ice lit up in a creamy gold that crept up the sides of the huge volcano, all the way to the top, where Erebus spewed plumes of sulfur-laden smoke into the sky.

As the weeks of the Antarctic spring wore on, the mountains that I'd seen earlier as solid, one-dimensional dark shapes against a canvas of vibrant color began to take on new depths because of the rising sun angle. As the light rose and stayed, I could see deeper into the Royal Society Range, the line of mountains across the frozen sea ice from McMurdo. The landscape became more complex. I could make out valleys and peaks I hadn't been aware of before. The effect was much like turning on an overhead light in a room where you've been reading quietly with only your bedside lamp beside you—troubling complexities appear so plainly in the harsher light; things once charmingly disguised become visible.

At the peak of the Antarctic summer season it is light twenty-four hours a day. The light is bright, sterile, technical, like the light in a hospital operating room. It is unavoidable light that actively seeks and annihilates corners of darkness and mystery. It was a shock to be out with friends, leaving McMurdo's coffeehouse near midnight, and have to blink into the brightness, shading my eyes with my hand. I might rise at 7:00 A.M. and it would be just as bright as when I'd gone to bed. To sleep, I put a blanket over my window to block the light. During this time of year, I needed sunglasses just to peer out my window onto the sea ice to check the weather conditions. One day I burned my eyes and had to wear, from that point on, two pairs of glasses—dense green glacier glasses and over them tinted ski goggles—in order to see without experiencing searing pain. Brightness began to overwhelm everything, illuminate everything. It became a light like water, washing over everything, washing everything down to its barest, clearest bones.

As Ruth, Donal Manahan, Tom Learned, and I made our way from Cape Evans back to McMurdo, over the flat sea ice bathed in yellow and pink, the sky around us continued to glow. In the sky behind Tent Island there were strange dark clouds against a fiery plum background mixed with cobalt and orange. The thin wispy clouds looked like letters, as if someone had lightly written some kind of careless script in the sky. I tried to make out a word. What could it be? *Fire? Mountain? Fountain? Fly?* A whispered suggestion. An incantation. We were all four so taken with the strange light that we stopped, got out, and took more pictures. Ruth posed there, standing with her back to Mount Erebus, the whole of the sky glowing pink and gold, her arms outstretched—from her fingertips on one side across her shoulders, along her other arm all the way to the fingertips on the other side—making a straight line just where the sea ice stopped and the mountain began, just where the horizon met the sky, so that the mountain itself seemed to ride upon her shoulders.

# THE SKY, THE EARTH,
# THE SEA, THE SOUL

I t was blowing so hard outside that the outhouse was rocking. Inside, there was brief relief from the wind and some relief, although not much, from the cold. I was at Siple Dome, a science camp on the West Antarctic Ice Sheet, where scientists were collecting samples of ancient ice to try to predict the course of global warming. I'd driven out on a snowmobile with scientist Kendrick Taylor to the Siple Dome drill site, where he was inspecting preparations for the season's project. Aside from the outhouse, the only two other places to get away from the howling wind and freezing cold were the drill site bar (named Little Alaska and housed in a musty, dark canvas jamesway), and the eerie, blue, silent ice trench where the ice samples were being stored.

I was in the outhouse not to get out of the wind, but to take a pee. It took me awhile, peeling off layer after layer of clothing. While engaged with straps and buckles and layers of nylon and fleece, I started to read the walls and remembered I'd been told to look for this outhouse—it was rather famous in Antarctica, traveling from field camp to field camp and gathering signatures and messages at every stop. It was a place where, year after year, scientists, drillers, other support workers, and visitors could leave their mark. The outhouse, and all the other buildings at Siple Dome, including the galley jamesway with its wooden Café Bubba marquee, the jamesways used for sleeping, for bathing, for the camp medic, and the one for the scientists' office space, would be dismantled at the conclusion of this particular science project and, if needed, moved somewhere else, say, from the West Antarctic Ice Sheet to the Shackleton Glacier, where the same huts would house a different team of scientists. This moveable feast of an outhouse was famous for its graffiti, which liberally covered its walls, in both neat and scrawling script, letters large and small, conveying messages profound and absurd.

> . . . Come, my friends.
> 'Tis not too late to seek a newer world.
> Push off, and sitting well in order smite
> The sounding furrows; for my purpose holds
> To sail beyond the sunset, and the baths
> Of all the western stars, until I die.
> It may be that the gulfs will wash us down;
> It may be we shall touch the Happy Isles,
> And see the great Achilles, whom we knew.
> Tho' much is taken, much abides; and tho'
> We are not now that strength which in old days
> Moved earth and heaven, that which we are, we are,—
> One equal temper of heroic hearts,
> Made weak by time and fate, but strong in will
> To strive, to seek, to find, and not to yield.

These were the unmistakable words of Ulysses, as written by the poet Tennyson, and also the words inscribed at the base of the statue of Robert Falcon Scott, whose bronze figure stands in a pretty square by the river Avon in Christchurch, New Zealand.

My eyes continued to roam the weathered plywood walls: "Polar exploration is at once the cleanest and most isolated way of having a bad time which has been devised." These words come from the introduction to *The Worst Journey in the World*, Apsley Cherry-Garrard's account of the Scott expedition. "Cherry" also covered in his account the journey from Scott's Cape Evans hut to Cape Crozier, where he, Edward Wilson, and "Birdie" Bowers wanted to collect newly laid emperor penguin eggs. When they returned, finally, after bitter nights in unbelievable storms—having had to sleep in reindeer hide sleeping bags frozen stiff with ice, having had their teeth split into pieces by the cold, having had to defecate in their trousers and shake the frozen shit loose—they were hardly recognizable as the men who'd left five weeks earlier. Of their return, Scott wrote in his diary: "The result of this effort is the appeal it makes to our imaginations as one of the most gallant stories of Polar History. That men should wander forth in the depth of a Polar night to face the most dismal cold and the fiercest gales in darkness is something new; that they should have persisted in this effort in spite of every adversity for five full weeks is heroic. It makes a tale for our generation which I hope may not be lost in the telling."

That they had done it for science made it all the nobler. "The British," wrote Antarctic historian Roland Huntford, "had an exalted view of science as moral uplift." *Dulce et decorum est pro scientia mori*, Antarctic historian and marine scientist Donal Manahan put it one evening during a presentation in McMurdo Station's galley: It is sweet and proper to die for science.

Another message on the outhouse wall, from Arctic explorer Fridjtof Nansen, read:

> People perhaps still exist who believe it is of no importance to explore the unknown polar regions. This, of course, shows ignorance. It is hardly necessary to mention here of what scientific import it is

that these regions should be thoroughly explored. The history of the human race is a continual struggle from darkness toward light. It is therefore, to no purpose to discuss the uses of knowledge. Man wants to know, and when he ceases to do so, he is no longer a man.

I had a feeling that this contribution must have come from a scientist, in response perhaps to such manly kidding as was revealed in the quip scribbled nearby: "Keep Antarctica Beautiful. Nuke a Beaker," *beaker* being the word used by nonscientists to refer, derogatorily, to scientists in Antarctica. Or perhaps "Nuke a Beaker" was not the chicken but the egg, a response to the assertion that intellectual acuity and imagination were the manliest of traits and that not to have them meant one was a wimp.

Near the Nansen quote on the wall I read this: "And now there came both mist and snow, / And it grew wondrous cold: / And ice, mast-high, came floating by, / As green as emerald." It was part of Samuel Taylor Coleridge's "The Rime of the Ancient Mariner," in which the mariner's ship gets blown off track, ending up in the horrible ice-choked southern seas, and the albatross comes to guide the ship to safer waters. When, out of boredom and anxiety, the mariner shoots the bird, the ship once again is beset in devilishly calm seas, the dead bird being hung around the mariner's neck as punishment.

The wall was also festooned with sex jokes. "Would you, could you, on a tower? I would, I could, I did." Near that was a cutaway picture of a huge ice drill, like the one towering outside, and the hole it was making in the ice sheet. The depths were numbered and labeled: "150 meters, coreplay; 250 meters, intercore; 430, coretus interruptus; 507, drill stuck, need giant tube of core jelly; 554.19, coregasm."

In Little Alaska, the tavern next door to the outhouse, a chest-high plywood bar served as the place where, at the end of the day, the drillers rested their elbows to sip their Danish bitters or beer. No proper tavern, it was a dirty, cold green canvas hut smelling of diesel fuel and cigarette smoke, the wind buffeting its thick plastic windows. The wood on the bar was carved and painted with jokes and quotes, just as in the outhouse, some nonsensical, some bizarre. "Maybe I'd sell you a chicken with poison interlaced with the meat." Or, "Find 'em, Fuck 'em and Forget 'em." Also carved deeply into the wood, with pen tips, screwdrivers, and pocket knives, was a long list of answers, made over time by many hands, to the question "How do we survive in this world?" *Sarcasm. Racism. Feminism. Patriotism. Environmentalism. Industrialism. Territorialism. Nepotism. Ethnocentrism. Anthropocentrism. Cynicism. Alcoholism. Isolationism. Orgasm. Paganism. Hedonism. Nudism. Anarchism. Sexism. Rugged Individualism.*

All this leaving of marks made me think of the words of the narrator in Ursula K. LeGuin's short story "Sur," the tale of a fictional group of South American women who venture to the South Pole in 1909. The women reach the pole (two years before Amundsen and Scott) but decide to leave no sign, no mark of their being there—no rock cairn, no flag, no pictures, no tent, no message to their King. They know this means their trek will go unnoted, unrecorded, ignored. They know and do not care. They did not go for science. They did not go for their country. They did not go to leave a mark. They went "simply to go and see. A simple ambition, I think," the narrator says, "and essentially a modest one."

At the Pole the narrator writes that there seemed no reason to leave a mark: "Anything we could do, anything we were, was insignificant, in that awful place." The story ends ironically with the birth of a child at the expedition base camp at the Bay of Whales, where the expedition members are safely picked up by their ship, the *Yelcho.* The child is named Rosa del Sur, the Compass Rose, and delivered without incident in the snug cave the women had built for themselves out of ice.

When visiting the South Pole, I found myself one evening in the snug recreation room underneath the station's big dome, a room strangely not unlike the Siple Dome outhouse. Dominated by a pool table and lounge chairs, the room had low, drink-ringed coffee tables littered with old magazines, and the walls were lined with plaques decorated with eagles, leaves, and stars. There were framed letters, awards, and commendations of all sorts.

It struck me as grand and heroic, romantic, noble, manly, and also sad and small. If the world could see this, I thought, the heart of all this desire, the recreation room at the South Pole, the southern axis of the planet Earth, this very room with its scrubby, cast-off furniture and walls bedecked with ribbons and trophies and granite slabs carved with bold capital letters—Hero, Struggle, God, King—what would they think? They might wonder what the race to the Pole was all about. There was no pot of gold here at the end of all that miserable trekking, just flat white all around, frozen solid miles and miles deep, just wind and cold and sky, and this ordinary little room, bedecked with prizes.

On the wall there was a framed copy of the book *The South Pole: An Account of the Norwegian Expedition in the* Fram *1910–1912*, by Roald Amundsen, inscribed by him in New York in 1925 with these words: "To My Comrades, The Brave Little Band That Promised In The Funchal Roads To Stand By Me In The Struggle For The South Pole. I Dedicate This Book."

There, in a frame, was a beige V-necked sweater, worn by Admiral Richard E. Byrd, U.S. Navy, on his historic flight over the South Pole in 1929. Byrd had written of that great accomplishment: "One gets there and that is about all there is for the telling. It is the effort to get there that counts." Alongside the Byrd sweater, in a playful attempt to point up the pomposity of the larger display, was a paint-spattered sweatshirt of an ordinary working man in a similar clear plastic box frame, with dog tags and the words: "Worn by Rod Jensen, during his historic winters at the South Pole Station."

There was a grim black-and-white picture of Amundsen, with his long nose, creased upper lip, and weary face, framed in the fur ruff of a huge parka hood. The severely compressed biography below it supplied the barest details: "1872–1928. First mate on the Belgica Expedition, the first expedition to pass an Antarctic winter. Started for the Pole from the Bay of Whales on October 19, 1911. Headed up the Axel Heiberg glacier, hitherto uncharted, setting off on what author Roland Huntford called at that time 'the last great terrestrial journey left to man.'"

Amundsen and his men traveled by dogsled and skis. They returned, dogs and men healthy, to the Bay of Whales on January 25, 1912. He spent 99 days on the trail. His dogs gained weight. "The goal was reached, the journey ended. I cannot say, though I know it would sound much more effective, that the object of my life was attained," he wrote. What he'd actually wanted was the North Pole, but he'd turned around on his way there in 1909 because it had been reached already, and he headed south to be the first at the South Pole instead. Of this turnaround, he wrote, "Can anything more topsy-turvy be imagined?"

Near the portrait of Amundsen was a black-and-white portrait of Scott, in a paper collar and tie and suit. He looked much softer than Amundsen, his face rounder, his eyes warmer. His years: 1868–1912. "Officer, scientist, gentleman," the biography below the portrait read. "Robert Falcon Scott made great the struggle rather than the goal. Frail and sickly as a child, he overcame physical infirmity to enter the Royal Navy and rise to the rank of Captain."

Scott and four fellow adventurers chosen to make the final bid to the Pole got to it just over a month after Amundsen, doggedly trudged back, with never enough to eat, each hiding his true condition from the others. They were found in their tent, Scott with his arm raised over one of his companions in some inexplicable gesture. One story says that when a rescuer tried to lower the arm, it snapped off in the cold with a sound like a gun blast. Scott's last words, inscribed in his journal and in the final letters he wrote to loved ones and expedition supporters, were couched in the most gentlemanly, most proper language, full of understatement and civility:

> I fear we must go and that it leaves the Expedition in a bad muddle.
> But we have been to the Pole and we shall die like gentlemen. . . .
> After all, we have given our lives for our country—we have actu-
> ally made the longest journey on record, and we have been the first
> Englishmen at the South Pole. . . . I do not regret this journey, which
> has shown that Englishmen can endure hardships, help one another,
> and meet death with as great a fortitude as ever in the past. . . . Had
> we lived, I should have had a tale to tell of the hardihood, endurance,
> and courage of my companions which would have stirred the heart
> of every Englishman. These rough notes and our dead bodies must
> tell the tale.

Among all the bombast of the displays I looked at, all the strut-ting and crowing, all the claims of being first, or best, or fastest, or longest, the most poignant of all the mementos spoke quietly and gave voice to something larger than domination and achievement. It spoke of things human and for all time, of pride and despair.

This one commemoration consisted of two photographs, the first an old, washed-out, hand-painted print of Poleheim, around it standing four Norwegians facing the flag, hatlesss in what must have been bitter, bitter cold, hands over their chests, chins high. Under it was written, "Presented to Amundsen Scott South Pole Station on the 60th Anniversary of Amundsen's attainment, on behalf of the Norwegian Geographical Society." Directly next to it, a print of the same old and hand-painted quality showed Scott and his party. An empty pair of skis and poles are planted in the foreground, Amund-sen's ghostly tent and the Norwegian flag are in the background, and the men are scattered in weird formation, two staring at the camera, one fumbling with his mittens, one bent toward Amundsen's tent as if about to look inside. The camera seems to have caught them un-posed. The photograph's caption reads, "Robert Falcon Scott's party at the South Pole on January 18, 1912, on behalf of the Norwegian Geographical Society, 1971, December 14."

The Norwegians presented the prints to the South Pole Station as a pair. The gift seems oddly cruel and ironic, as if intended to point out the vast gulf between Amundsen's success and Scott's failure. Upon arrival at the Pole, Scott had written in his journal, "Great God, this is an awful place, and terrible enough for us to have laboured to it without the reward of priority." Their sense of defeat was absolutely evident in the photograph, so starkly the opposite of its Norwegian counterpart.

The displays at the South Pole, the graffiti in the Siple Dome outhouse, and the carved messages in the Siple Dome bar reveal that Antarctica is an undeniably masculine space. Indeed, the language and images used to tell the story of Antarctica have until recently been *thoroughly* masculine, colored not only by the early, exclusively male presence on the continent, but also by the early association of the military with Antarctic exploration. Early book titles included *Antarctic Assualt, Man Against the Desolate Antarctic, Assault on the Unknown, Strong Men South, The Siege of the South Pole*—works that spur the imagination to conjure the landscape as a kind of hell, the scientists as heroes, the soldiers as lone knights.

While men had been busy attacking, laying siege to, assaulting, pitting their wills against, being strong in and strengthened by, dominating, proving their patriotism in, and getting themselves frostbitten and killed in Antarctica, as well as writing all about it, what were women doing? From what you might be able to read about women in Antarctica, you'd be led to only one answer—nothing. The popular Reader's Digest coffee-table book, *Antarctica: The Extraordinary History of Man's Conquest of the Frozen Continent*, claims to be the complete story of this unique place. For all but two of its 320 pages, however, it leaves discussion of women out, except in the chapter titled "The Women They Left Behind," a short essay about the unsung wives of the Antarctic explorers.

The truth is that women *have* wanted to go to Antarctica, they *have* had adventurism in their blood, just as they've had it in their blood to travel the globe as men do, even, in our time, to enter space. But they've found it difficult to get to Antarctica. There is another side to the masculine history of Antarctica, a women's history, but it's been lying low, as women's history often does, unremarked upon in the bigger book of human accomplishment.

It wasn't until 1974 that a woman was *allowed* to stay the winter at a U.S. station in Antarctica. The U.S. Navy, which was responsible for U.S. doings in Antarctica up until the end of 1997, felt that letting women, even scientists, set forth upon the continent would bring with it insurmountable difficulties, such as the problem of having to provide separate bathroom facilities for men and women, and the problem, considered grave, of having to protect women from the danger of being raped by lonely, sex-starved soldiers and scientists.

"There are some things women don't do. They don't become Pope or President or go down to the Antarctic," seemed to be the overwhelming sentiment. It was voiced in 1947 by Harry Darlington, as he tried to dissuade his bride, Jennie Darlington, from accompanying him on the Ronne Antarctic expedition, a journey Jennie writes about in her book *My Antarctic Honeymoon*. Darlington is also famous for his response to the question "What do you miss most in Antarctica? Fresh food?" No, he said, scandalously, not even women, but "temptation." Admiral Richard E. Byrd imagined Antarctica as a sacred, femaleless place, free of temptation, a holy land: "The whole of Antarctica might be referred to as a mighty cathedral of glittering ice and painted sky erected by the Lord's own hand. Far from the turmoil and temptations of the world, it is the ideal retreat for those who find a more intimate touch with the infinite greatness and goodness."

The first woman to set foot in Antarctica is said to have been Caroline Mikkelsen, the wife of a Norwegian whaling captain. On

February 20, 1935, she is said to have stepped ashore (no doubt in a voluminous dress) for a short time near the present location of Australia's Davis Station, on the Antarctic Peninsula. After she looked around, she was taken back to the ship. The next women to get anywhere near the continent were the wife, daughter, and two female friends of shipping magnate Lars Christensen. Although the women never got off the ship, the landmark Four Ladies Bank, just off the Ingrid Christensen Coast, was named after them.

Next, in the late 1940s, were Edith Ronne and Jennie Darlington, who accompanied their husbands to Stonington Island near the Antarctic Peninsula. They spent a year in Antarctica, as part of an ill-fated expedition, becoming the first women ever to live on the continent.

While the U.S. Navy continued to stall with lame excuses about bathroom facilities, other countries were letting women work and live on Antarctic bases. Four Argentinean professors, for instance, did hydraulic research on the continent in 1968 and 1969. This first seemed to open a door for others, as 1969 saw, finally, the first U.S. National Science Foundation–funded all-female research team, headed by geochemist Lois Jones from Ohio State University. Jones had originally resigned herself to doing all her research about Dry Valleys lakes from her lab in Ohio, as, because of her gender, she was officially banned from the continent. When she and her research team did arrive, they were paraded around by the navy as part of a publicity stunt—even sent to the South Pole to meet navy brass and have their photographs taken: the first women *ever* to set foot on the ice at the South Pole. The headlines that accompanied the stories declared, "Powderpuff Explorers Invade South Pole." Reporters asked questions about lipstick, hair, and the difficulty of personal hygiene in such a harsh environment.

Like Jones, Dr. Mary Alice McWhinnie waited a long while to enter the continent. An American expert on krill, she did research in Antarctica for ten years, cruising the oceans just off the continent, without setting foot on land, on forbidden territory. When she finally was allowed to land in 1974, McWhinnie became the first woman ever to head an Antarctic research station, having been appointed the chief science officer at McMurdo, where, in another first, she spent the Antarctic winter, along with her required "assistant," Sister Mary Odile Cahoon, a biologist and nun. The two women have become mythic—the middle-aged scientist and the nun—two maiden aunts, asexual, motherly, and nurturing. Perhaps those in charge reasoned that they were the perfect women to set the stage for others to follow—they wouldn't disturb the sexual dynamics of the base, and they could provide motherly and sisterly companionship.

Other women followed, breaking down barriers: in 1979 Michelle Rainey became the first woman selected to be the year-round doctor at the South Pole; in 1993 the first all-women's expedition reached the Pole on foot, from the Weddell Sea, and in the year 2001 a team made up of Minnesota school teacher and polar explorer Ann Bancroft (also the leader of the 1993 all-women's expedition) and Norwegian teacher Liv Arneson crossed the entire continent on foot. Perhaps most remarkable, South Pole doctor Jerri Nielsen's dramatic account of treating herself for breast cancer during an Antarctic winter not only made headlines worldwide, but also became the best-selling book, *Ice Bound*, as well as a movie starring Susan Sarandon, bringing a woman's story of Antarctic heroism into the popular imagination for the first time.

The navy's insistence on keeping women out of Antarctica until the mid-1970s is something of a curiosity. Why all that trouble to keep women out? The answer is both simple and complex: to preserve a space, a womanless space, a clean, pure, celibate, priestly space, a space like an ice-bound Eden before the fall, for the uninterrupted reproduction of that set of values and beliefs that are so clearly on display at the South Pole and in the Siple Dome outhouse and bar. The space being preserved is space for the reproduction of all that we know of as masculine, so that heroic expeditions like Scott's, like Amundsen's, and like others that came later, could be re-enacted, endlessly, thereby protecting something elemental from change, from time, from history—what it means to be a man, and by elaboration, what it means to be a human being. At stake was nothing less than the definition, albeit an extremely limited one, of our very being—*Who* are we?

But things in Antarctica have changed, drastically. Recent unofficial reports suggest that of the thousand or so carpenters, plumbers, electricians, scientists, laboratory technicians, administrators, secretaries, janitors, cooks, pilots, firefighters, doctors, dentists, nurses, mountaineers, heavy equipment operators, recreation specialists, and others working at McMurdo Station each austral summer, at least 40 percent are female, up from 0 percent in the early 1970s. Informal interviews revealed that most men at McMurdo, even those who'd worked in Antarctica twenty seasons, who'd been present at the beginning of the revolution, thought that having men and women at McMurdo normalized the town and made it a better place to work and live. "Without women around," said one clean-cut male engineer, "men are pigs." It all brings to mind the Stephen Crane short story "The Bride Comes to Yellow Sky," about the marshal's bride who, amid much controversy, comes to live with her new husband in a turn-of-the century frontier town, and in the end exerts a civilizing influence on the Wild West outpost.

The outhouse was still rocking with wind, still bitterly chilling, the seat frosty, the walls glistening with frozen crystals. I was in the process of redressing. But, *wait*, there was an empty space on the wall. I, *too*, could leave my mark! What would I say, what would I pass down for all to read? Shelley? Tennyson? The Ancient Mariner? Scott? I thought again of the narrator of LeGuin's story, and what she says of their decision to leave no mark at the pole: "I was glad even then that we left no sign there, for some man longing to be the first might come some day, and find it, and know then what a fool he had been, and break his heart." The "backside of heroism," says

LeGuin's narrator, is "often rather sad; women and servants know that. They know also that the heroism may be no less real for that. But achievement is smaller than men think. What is large is the sky, the earth, the sea, the soul."

In the end, I left no mark on the outhouse wall. In fact, Antarctica may bear no imprint of me at all, but the place itself will have marked me, seared itself upon me like an icy hot brand. I zipped up my parka and stepped out into the cold, sweeping, flat white of the ice.

# SIPLE DOME

At Siple Dome the winter had created a major catastrophe. The roof covering the enormous ice trench that had been dug as a storage facility for the ice samples from the previous year's research had nearly caved in. It was now groaning under ten feet of snow, all of which needed to be shoveled off before the roof could be properly repaired. The whole of the camp was employed for a week shoveling, which created an atmosphere of comedy. The shovel became the D-1, a joke that referenced the larger pieces of heavy excavating equipment, the D-4s, D-7s, and D-9s, that usually handled snow removal in Antarctica.

The problem with science in Antarctica, remarked Kendrick Taylor, whose science project was in danger of being ruined by the caving-in trench, is that it was 80 percent this—logistics, that is, shoveling snow—and only 20 percent "real" science. Taylor, like everyone else, was sweating and breathless, his dark beard full of frost, his freckles come alive from the sun. The problem with science in general, he added, was that it was slow. It would take four to five years for Taylor to get any kind of an answer to his question: what was happening in the Southern Pacific Ocean 150,000 years ago. "It just happens," he explained, "that the glaciology and climatology of Siple Dome is such that it is one of the best places to collect a record of environmental conditions for a large area of the Southern Pacific." Taylor hoped that this information would tell him something about climate change today—are we on the edge of catastrophic global warming, or are we not?—and also provide clues about the role of the South Pacific as a driver of abrupt climate change, something scientists have thought was driven exclusively by the oceans of the North Atlantic.

Climate change can happen faster than we think, he said, re-peating what I'd heard before from other scientists in Antarctica. He joked: "We say that climate change can happen faster than it takes some of our graduate students to finish their degrees." The heady fuel for the project at Siple Dome was the promise that, in the end, we'd be able to know with some certainty when the big meltdown or the new ice age was coming, and prepare ourselves adequately for it. With his dark eyes and wild dark hair, I imagined Taylor as a Gypsy fortune-teller, his crystal ball the long, clear tubes of ice drawn from deep down in the well of frozen earth.

Taylor's goal was to collect 1,000 meters of thick ice core from Siple Dome, a hump in the thick ice sheet that covered West Ant-arctica. The ice at Siple Dome had such high resolution, Taylor ex-plained, that scientists could count annual layers of ice; they could analyze the ice's chemistry, and even get an idea of the temperature of the surrounding environment during the time the ancient ice was new.

In the ice trench built to house the settling ice cores, men with chain saws were at work deepening the cavern by another ten feet, correcting the mistake of the year before. I was helping by taking the two-foot-square blocks of ice out of the way of the chain sawers, rough young men who were on contract with PICO, a drilling company that did much of its work in the Arctic. I piled the ice blocks onto a wooden sled, which was then towed out of the trench by snowmobile. I followed the snowmobile and unloaded the blocks out of the way, somewhere in the sun.

The trench itself was huge. Walking into it, I imagined myself walking down into the tombs of the ancient Egyptians, down eerily lit corridors of stone into the belly of a pyramid. In this long, deep tunnel, the walls glowed deep blue and the air was stale and frozen. In the cave every other word the chain sawers said was "fuck." Some were stripped down to their bare chests, revealing their thin wiriness and their muscled arms. Cigarettes dangled from their lips. The chain saws screamed and caught, screamed and caught. They were racing each other to see who could cut the most blocks. As they cut deeper and deeper they sunk lower and lower, their sweaty heads soon level with the ledge of ice that ran the length of the trench. As I stood gazing down at them, I imagined Egyptian slaves cutting blocks of stone.

They all had hangovers from the night before. Even in this dense, ice-walled cellar I could smell their acrid bodies. Clouds of steam rose from their quick breath, and ice smoke rose in crystals from the chain saws. A tangle of lighting cords wove around them. "Fuck. What the fuck is up with my fucking chain saw," one swore. They complained out loud about "the head beaker dude" who didn't want anymore of this "seat-of-the-pants crap" they said, mimicking him, slapping their butts. The "head beaker dude" was an engineer who was trying to solve the problem of the caved-in roof by calculating the density of the snow that was likely to accumulate on the roof over the next winter, so that the roof could be rebuilt strongly enough, so, as Taylor put it, "I won't have to be standing around on the Fourth of July in America worrying that my ice cores are being crushed in Antarctica."

Among this crew of chain sawers were the two twenty-something men from the PICO drilling team who, just after their arrival, entered the camp galley on Halloween night naked except for fur loincloths. Left to their own devices that night, they were still drinking tequila in the morning, one of them vomiting outside in the snow, one of them, or both, having written something indecipherable in shit and vomit on the outhouse wall. Hard characters. Antarctica appealed to such tough cases, partly because it seemed a place away from one's "real" life.

There were also those who appreciated Antarctica not so much as a place to escape, but as a place where one could experience a state of egalitarianism not readily found elsewhere. A friend told me the story of Prince Edward of Great Britain visiting the New Zealanders at Scott Base. When the prince sat down at the dinner table he was introduced as "Edward," to which the response was, "Hello, Edward, how are you?" Down here, many asserted, it didn't matter how much money you made or what your degree was in or how smart you were. Everyone was in the same boat and you'd better damned well learn to get along—even with the drunk guys in the loincloths.

On one of my last evenings at Siple Dome, I attended a party in the canvas staff tent, where, when I entered, I found about a dozen red-cheeked people slumped comfortably into piles of pillows and blankets. They were knitting hats, playing cards, trying to force a tune out of an old squeeze box, passing around a bottle of Scotch. It looked a little like what I imagine the interior of a Bedouin tent might look, but instead of being spread with carpets and camel hide, each cot had been walled off with expertly hung military-issue blankets and each cubbyhole was adorned with private knickknacks and photographs. The blankets had been pinned back for the evening, the private spaces opening up and creating an ultimately domestic, cozy feel.

I took a seat on the floor and was offered a book, along with the suggestion that, as the writer, I read from it. It was a collection of Jack London stories and I chose "Love of Life." As I read on into the night, knitting needles slowed, eyes began to droop, and bodies began to slump, exhausted, into the clumps of pillows and blankets around them. I finished the story the following night, sitting with a handful of others around the warm kerosene stove in the doctor's canvas hut.

The story's two main characters, who are gold miners in the wilds of the Klondike, come across hard times. They end up separated and starving. One man, after crawling for days on hands and knees, finally comes to his friend's dead body and has to decide whether to eat from his friend's bones. He doesn't. He crawls on and eventually gets saved. But he becomes fat, a hoarder of food, hungry and forever unable to assuage his ravenous cravings. His worst nightmare, starvation, becomes his obsession—his worst fear takes over his life. He overcame death through some kind of faith, through endurance and love of life, through instinct, but now that he was through the worst of it, his psyche had taken over, keeping him prisoner to the fear that it would happen again. Rather than love life now, he puts all his energies toward precaution.

The story made me think about my own fears—the worst being that I was broken and unlovable. That fear had clung to me all my life, and I'd nurtured it, the way a body, with its own blood, unwittingly nurtures a leech clamped on, undetected inside a shoe or up a pant leg. Like the man in the story who wanted never to starve again but made himself forever hungry, I wanted to be fed by love, but in some ways continued to make myself forever bereft, out of fear—fear that the person I loved wouldn't love me back, fear that the supply of love was limited, that it would run out. The man in the story was sane, the narrator tells us, and would eventually get over his fear, but in the meantime, he lined his pockets, his mattress, his pillow cases, with food. I had another chance, now, with Ruth, to lay down all those old, protective habits, to open my heart to something new, to take another risk on life. What would come of it, whether I'd be able to do it, I didn't yet know.

＊

When I left Siple Dome, it was with relief. I learned later that scientists and workers there had nicknamed it Siple *Doom*. It seemed full of excess, with the near, but not quite counterbalancing weight of wholesome domesticity on the other end. There was the drill site bar with its violent graffiti, the explosive, just-contained energy of angry young men besotted with booze, the roar of the heavy equipment, the chain saws, the isolation, the eerie ice trench that seemed forever to me like a tomb, and there was the antithesis of all that—enthusiastic science, people sitting around at night knitting or reading stories aloud or jitterbugging on the plywood galley floor to '50s music blaring from a boom box, the smell and taste of fresh breads and cakes, the simple, sensual pleasure of the sun, the company of men and women who appreciated the value of a hard day's work. It seemed as if these counterforces were vying for position.

Every field camp has its own identity, its own energy, Kendrick Taylor had told me. Later in the summer this one would change, he assured me. How it would change, which way it might lean, I was never to know. Buckled into the red nylon webbing of the C-130, I twisted around to peer out the tiny porthole near my seat and watched as the camp became smaller out the window, changing its nature the farther I got from it—the tent city neatly fixed in a circle with its colorful domes of nylon, the jamesways lined up neatly facing a carefully manicured airstrip, the road to the drill site clearly, neatly marked. It all looked so well-planned and efficient from the air. But down in those flimsy canvas shelters, I knew, were people, humans, whose complexity and unpredictability made hash of the tidy design I could see from the air—they were down there being joyful, proud, funny, stupid, imaginative, fearful, drinking too much, delivering desperate messages in the calligraphy of their own smeared feces, solving the world's mysteries and creating new ones.

# THE ICE KING

Like many Antarctic veterans, Rocky Ness, in certain moods, could speak quite nostalgically about the old days, meaning 1970 or thereabouts, when being in Antarctica meant you might as well have been on Mars. Antarctica then was so distant from the rest of the world that even if you'd wanted to you couldn't have picked up a phone and dialed home. "When that plane left in February that was it," said Ness, with a quick chop of his hand to indicate the utter finality of that departure.

Ness has spent more time in Antarctica than any other human on earth. In McMurdo they called him the Ice King. A short man with reddish brown hair, a trim reddish brown beard, and a pleasingly round head, he had a smile like Lewis Carroll's Cheshire cat, a smile that reached from ear to ear, but was oddly unconvincing. His eyes were milky blue, his speech quick and full of ironic twists and sly, self-deprecating remarks.

On this day, he leaned back in his desk chair, talking half to himself, looking out the window of his small, stuffy office. The best thing they had in the old days to communicate with the larger world was a Ham Shack, which housed a ham radio setup you had to make an appointment to use. In a ham radio patch, the radio operator in McMurdo put out a general call to anyone in the United States willing to assist with the connection. Once a fellow ham operator was located, that person, sitting at his or her radio console in, say, Denton, Texas, picked up a telephone and dialed your parents or your girlfriend in San Diego. Once that connection was established the ham operator in Texas hooked your friend on the phone up to the radio and you could proceed. Rocky's parents became so familiar with ham radio routine that they still talk to him this way, even over the modern telephone lines that seamlessly link them today: "Hi . . . over . . . Things are going fine here. Over. We're mowing the lawn . . . over."

In the middle of winter back in the old days, Rocky said, sometimes the radio just wouldn't cut it. Only ten people a week could make a call. It was scratchy and crackly. "I couldn't quite hear what that was . . . over." You could talk for ten minutes at best. *But now look at what I've got!* He swiveled around and gestured at the elaborate computer setup on his desk. It had a video application and speakers. He could now have a free video conference with home any time he wanted. His father called him every other day. With a sigh, as if it was just all too much, he said, "I can call and check the balance in my Fidelity mutual fund toll-free, right now! *Get outta here!*"

He swiveled his chair back, and looked again out one of the windows to the murky blend of snow and dirt outside, to the telephone and electric poles strung with wires, the roofs of the other buildings. Behind him was the wide expanse of the frozen Ross Sea and the magnificent mountains. Out the window Rocky could keep an eye on what, as Operations Manager, he was responsible for at McMurdo. This time of year his most important job was overseeing the preparation of the ice runway. Directly in his view were the yellow bulldozers, the graders, and the McMurdo Station fire truck, all being used to make the ice runway that would handle the landings of the massive airplanes bringing scientists, more workers, and supplies. Although the airplanes would mostly be C-111s and C-130s, they would also include the hulking C-5, the largest plane in the world. The runway, which would be complete with a passenger waiting terminal (a metal building hauled out on runners), a galley for VIPs, restrooms, a control tower, and other necessary outbuildings, constituted McMurdo's main chore at this time of year, requiring the concerted, round-the-clock labor of most of the station.

To the left out the window, far, far away, past the colorful dots of the machines working back and forth over the ice, one could just make out the dim humps of Black Island and White Island, and beyond that, invisible, the long way to the South Pole. To the right out the window would be the dark fins of several islands now jutting up out of the frozen sea ice, ice that later in the season would turn into open ocean. Much later in the season, Rocky might be able to see from his window an iceberg float into view, or watch the National Science Foundation research vessel the *Nathaniel B. Palmer* park itself in Winter Quarters Bay. It was only early September and the colors washing over the ice and the mountains were still subtle—apricot, jade, and lavender.

"You just can't feel cut off down here anymore," Rocky said, sounding decidedly dismayed. He went on, expressing a paradoxical gratefulness for the technology, such as electronic mail, that allowed him to communicate with his mother on a regular basis, and nostalgia for the days when if you wanted to you could go to Antarctica and be away, be far enough away to be out of touch. You could, if you wanted to, hide. But now, since technology came to McMurdo, news tracked you down, hounded and haunted you. Antarctica was no longer an excuse for anything, for not answering phone calls, for letting your subscriptions lapse, for losing touch, for being out of the loop. Geologist Peter Webb remarked one day that when he first began working in Antarctica in the 1950s, the people around him tended to be "escapees and deniers of the truth." Now, he said, people who chose to work in Antarctica tended to be more adventurous, more community-oriented and less misanthropic. It is no longer such a safe haven for escape artists, for those fleeing their losses and fears.

Rocky arrived in Antarctica in 1980, when he was twenty-four, to work at Palmer Station, on the Antarctic Peninsula. He'd been a water plant mechanic, a facilities engineer, a station manager, and now, at McMurdo, Operations Manager. "I haven't worked anywhere else in seventeen years! In fact the only place I've lived for any length of time is here. When people ask me where I'm from I'm tempted to say Antarctica . . ." He looked puzzled for a moment, as if that was somehow hitting home in a way it previously hadn't. "This *is* kind of home," he said, twisting the cap of a pen in his fingertips, "which makes me feel weird sometimes because this is a place people leave screaming and never wanting to come back to . . . this has kind of turned into what I am."

The elaborate plaque honoring him for so many years of Antarctic service is a hefty square of thick, dark wood with a triangular frame on top for a folded American flag. The lower portion has several ceremonial certificates and medals under glass, including his winter-over medal, with gold, silver, and bronze bars next to it. One of the certificates reads: "In the name of the people by the people and for the people of the United States of America, in the name of all those who have proudly served in Antarctica, I present to you the Navy's most honored and cherished emblem, the Ensign of the United States of America." The flag presented with the award had flown for one month on the topmost flagpole at McMurdo Station, Antarctica. The award was signed, "D. P. Lilly, Officer in Charge, U.S. Naval Support Force, Antarctica."

"Wherever you go, there you are," a saying connected to '80s science-fiction hero Buckaroo Bonzai, appeared in numerous and unexpected places in Antarctica. On the wall behind the phone at the research camp at Lake Hoare in the Dry Valleys, there it was: "Wherever you go, there you are." On the bumper of one of McMurdo's orange pickup trucks. On the side of a filing cabinet in the office of a National Science Foundation administrator. At the South Pole on a wall in a dusty corner above a cluttered desk. Those who pasted that sticker to their cabinets or walls were acknowledging that in Antarctica you're at the mercy of time and geography. Wherever you go, there you are, for that moment. The almost cultish repetition of this postmodern proverb might indicate that, despite technologies that have changed our sense of space and time, we humans still have a strong desire for groundedness in place. We want to be rooted; we want to be somewhere real. The saying, "Wherever you go, there you are," seems also to be an acknowledgment that wherever you go, of course, you take places and people from the past with you. In other words, you can't escape who you are. Wherever you go, there *you* are, facing yourself again in the mirror.

All around McMurdo, *wherever you went* there were images of people's sacred places—posters, pictures from calendars, postcards, and glossy squares cut from magazines. There were pictures of fall in New England, pink-rose-petal-strewn garden paths, fields of red poppies. Above a desk would be a picture of a tent in a green mountain pass full of Indian paintbrush and white mountain daisies. In a building full of narrow paths through mazes of shelves stocked with electrical parts, you'd turn a corner and there would be fish swimming in a coral reef, open sea, docks lined with tugs and pleasure craft. There seemed in Antarctica to be a tension between these two poles: the technology that worked at making place less important, along with a Zen-like acceptance of this homelessness, and, on the other hand, people's absolute devotion to the places they came from and would return to, along with a fierce longing for this kind of *actual* home in the world.

The kind of technology that allowed Rocky Ness, the Ice King, to talk to his financial broker from his desk in Antarctica has a way of smudging the boundaries of the present, and when that happens we are always potentially not where we are but already somewhere else. A friend who was treated for breast cancer underwent magnetic resonance imaging (MRI) several times. She fought off the eeriness of the machine, a claustrophobic tube, by humming to herself. The machine works by rearranging the protons in your hydrogen atoms, taking them 90 to 180 degrees off their center axis by bombarding them with radio frequencies. The radio frequency is then turned off and, as the tissues relax, the protons snap back into place at different rates. All this unsettledness. It is like being rearranged at the very core.

Geography and the natural cycles that are part of it have indelibly shaped our human sense of space and time. We know, for instance, what it feels like to be far away from someone or some place that we love. We know it from the ache in our hearts, from our long-distance phone bills and the letters we write and send, from how long (down to the minute) it will take that person to drive or fly or walk to us. We know *who we are* by this—by this feeling of longing for what is far away and our feeling of joy and fullness for what is dear and near. By this feeling we know we are alive, we know we are in connection with other human beings and to time and space. You might say that love and space and time depend upon one another for meaning, that they mutually illuminate one another. You might say we know *who* we are by knowing *where* we are, and vice versa.

*Who* are we? *Where* are we? These were two of Thoreau's questions, as he contemplated life on his way up the sides of Mount Ktaadn, the fiercest landscape he knew. He believed that these questions were related. He believed that who we are individually and collectively is related to where we are geographically and perhaps even cosmically.

The desire for a place we can go where no one can find us, where we can start anew, is a yearning to give oneself over to the power of time, of distance, of geography. The nostalgia that some, like Rocky Ness, have for Antarctica's olden days might be an expression of a desire for place to matter. People want it to make a difference in their lives that they are at the South Pole. They want to be able to think that a place like Antarctica might change them somehow, make them stronger, wiser, more enlightened. But in today's wired world, where no matter where you go you seem to be connected to who you were when you were somewhere else, that sense of hope for a geographical difference is continually compressed.

What happens then? What happens when the pull to belong to a certain place, in a certain time, is constantly undone by technology so ubiquitous that you cannot avoid it, even in Antarctica? What happens to the human heart when you can sit, like Rocky, at your desk in Antarctica and talk to your father, who is out mowing the lawn in Minnesota, sweat staining his white T-shirt in the small of his back? You can hear the lawnmower engine throttle back, and the clink of ice in a glass of lemonade as you look across at the Transantarctic Mountains and the path to the South Pole. What happens when the heart's wild and natural desirings for a place to rest, for a home in the world, are repeatedly unmet?

What he wanted to do in the beginning, Rocky said, was to arrange his life so that he could travel, and he has. During his summers off from work in Antarctica he has traveled to South America, to Southeast Asia, to Africa. He wanders. He doesn't worry about details, about hotels, about airplanes. He lets those things happen. But, strangely, it doesn't satisfy him much anymore. "I need a place," he said. "If there's anything that's tearing me up inside it's lack of an address. I want a place I know I can go back to, to settle in, to stay. All this traveling I do . . . I see a place and think, I could live *here*, and later I'll see another wonderful, beautiful, incredible place and I think, I could live *here*!" Right now, as it stands, he says, "My permanent address is not even three dimensional. It's in cyberspace."

# VISIBLE PROOFS

E dward Wilson's many drawings of Antarctica chart the story of
a love affair, a deeply felt and growing devotion to the actual
world, a growing hunger for connection and understanding, a devotion to the idea of love itself. As Wilson once put it, "The hidden
things of God are understood and clearly seen in things created."

In Antarctica, I felt a kinship with Wilson and was inspired by
him. I took pastels, paper, and watercolor paints and brushes with
me to Antarctica. Lacking experience with these tools, I did my best
and found, to my surprise, that drawing and painting in the crude
way I could manage helped me see the "hidden things" Wilson spoke
of; drawing helped me pay attention to Antarctica in a way I might
not have as a writer thinking in words alone.

Crossing over the bridge between the world of the word and
the world of color and line deepened my vision. I watched more
keenly for patterns in the ice and sky, I was alert to the presence
of shadows and the most minute gradations in color, I kept an eye

out for unlikely shapes and strove to locate the detail that would be the key to the essence of the thing—the glacier edge, the waves of sculpted snow that lay upon the ice, the backbone of the mountains, the tracks of penguins. And because I was untrained in watercolors or pastels, I wasn't influenced by any allegiance to rule or form—I was completely, joyfully naive, a beginner, turning out sketches that any true artist would call primitive at best, but that served to open for me another way of seeing and knowing.

Some of Wilson's pictures give voice only to sky and rock and frozen sea, landscape with no sign of humans. Others situate humans precariously amid this wild grandeur, as in one picture from what we might call a bird's-eye view, looking down Observation Hill, a steeply sided hump near McMurdo Station, upon two miniscule figures crossing a wide flat sea, approaching Hut Point, the background full of blue shadow sweeping across the frozen plain of sea ice.

Other Wilson pictures focus closely on his expedition mates and their trials. One sketch depicts men huddled together in a tiny Scott tent (a peaked canvas tent with a center pole), another depicts men leading ponies by their rope halters through a storm. *The Last of the Dogs* may be one of the most moving. It shows a darkly drawn figure walking away from a spot in the immediate and invisible foreground of the sketch. Leading up to the spot are two sets of tracks—human tracks and dog tracks. The tracks leading away are those of only the man. The sky looms large. The land is flat. A small tent stands in the distance. The sketch depicts the intentional killing of the last of Scott's sled dogs, which at a certain planned point became unnecessary for the journey. Wilson's pictures go on and on, hundreds of them, creating a portrait of Wilson himself—passionate, precise, mystical—as much as they create a portrait of an inexplicable, brutal, and beautiful land.

One of the many interesting things about Wilson is the tug-of-war over whether the man was an artist, or was mainly a scientist. Was he drawing and painting in the service of beauty and grace and imagination, or in the service of truth and accuracy? Wilson's paintings fetch high prices at auctions of Antarctic memorabilia, and are one of the prize holdings of the Scott Polar Research Institute in Cambridge, England. Many scientists and scholars, however, seem to regard the paintings as somewhat irrelevant and quaint. "Pretty," is how one evaluator put it. Their scientific value, on the other hand, is lauded. Wilson's paintings give us a lasting record of fact, scientists and scholars say. They accurately portray color, shape, distance, and mathematical measurement. The pictures are more valued as data, it seems, than as expressions of feeling, moments of ecstasy or experiences of the sublime.

Only a little is known about what Wilson really thought about his art and art in general. He was a man of few words. *Res non verba*—Do, Don't Talk—was his family motto. He did give some advice for others who wished to draw Antarctica. In his May 31, 1911, lecture in the hut at Cape Evans, reproduced in the journal of his companion Griffith Taylor, he said: "Remember that nature relieves everything by shadow and colour, but not by *lines*." He said himself that "Accuracy rather than the making of pictures," was his main concern in Antarctica. Don't scribble, he said. Don't scribble in the clouds. Don't scribble in mountains. Don't adopt mannerisms. Most of all, look. "You can't," he advised, "overdo the exercise of your power of 'seeing' and down here the shades are so subtle that you get very good practice."

About Wilson's gift for accuracy, one expedition mate, Frank Debenham, writes: "For here was an artist of first-rate quality as to technique, who drew only truth, and refused to let his imagination guide his pencil; who pleased us by skillful drawings of what he saw, but denied us the keener pleasure of seeing on paper what he thought." Debenham chalks this up to Wilson's "devotion to duty" and his "iron control over his own feelings." Accuracy, Scott himself said in his journal, was what Wilson was all about. "His sketches are most astonishingly accurate. I have tested his proportions by actual angular measurement and found them correct."

Many of Wilson's original sketches are actually quite rough; just shapes and shadings with the colors jotted in for later work. In one sketch of Hut Point and new ice, with two figures in the middle dwarfed by all that is around them, he scribbled in the colors: "Yellow light all over. Purple dark lines, vivid green (in the upper left by the mountains). Palest green and lemon yellow (along the top of the mountain range). Slice of rose pink. Rosepink green. New ice. Dark brown. Gray. Brilliant brilliant (down the middle where the sun is shining on the ice). All very smooth ice." It would seem odd to call these early sketches "accurate," except to say the drawings evoke "accurately" what it feels like to pitch a tent in a blizzard, needles of snow stinging one's face and blistering one's hands, or what it feels like to hunker down in a tent in the middle of a howling wilderness, your only warmth a cookstove the size of a shoebox, or the awe and comfort one feels standing alone on the top of a breathlessly white peak in the midst of a deep night embraced by the pulsing lights of aurora australis. Perhaps the accuracy Wilson was after in these pictures was something other than the right color or correct line—deep emotion.

On the other hand, other of Wilson's pictures are *very technically* accurate and their value depends upon that; for example, Wilson's sketch of a panorama of the landward approach to the Beardmore Glacier, sketched from forty miles away on December 1, 1911, or his breathtaking drawing of a parahelia, sketched on November 14, 1911, at approximately 11 P.M. In the end, Wilson's own ecstatic voice dramatically erases any doubt over whether the man was engaged only in copying down data or was, in fact, reaching deeply into the unknown, seeking to lift the veil between the seen and the unseen. One of his journal entries reads:

> My pictures are the realization of little things that have been treasured up in my mind, little traits of character picked up crumb by crumb in fields and in hedgerows, at last pieced together and put into the form of something living—the realization of every happy day

I have spent on the hills is in the picture of a stoat I chanced to see, in the snakes; in that little head and one eye is all the fascinating quickness and supple gracefulness of all the snakes I have known, and I have never lost a chance of trying to know them better; the whole concentrated beauty of that glorious Norwegian forest at midnight is what I see in the picture of the sparrow-hawk's nest.

Was Wilson a dutiful realist or an artist/scientist of special sensitivity and vision? The answer may never be a simple one—Wilson's talents and his art may continue to be unsettling. Although he was not technically a late Victorian, he and his expedition mates surely inherited the anti-Romantic values of that age—nationalism, heroism, masculinity, and realism. Wilson's art is unsettling for many possible reasons: because his art gave voice to the absolute otherness of Antarctica, in an age when the land's otherness was exactly what was being conquered by man; because Antarctica was no place for the effeminate poet, only a place for the masculine hero bending against the wind; because Wilson was trying to give voice to competing understandings, ways of seeing the world that he had reconciled but those around him had not. For Wilson, the concepts of God, Art, and Science were not incompatible.

Although the writings of his expedition mates convey a sense of Wilson as unusually pious, in fact, Wilson, whose faith was a mix of Anglican, Quaker, and medieval mystic, was averse to organized religion, disdainful of religious hypocrisy, and he held unorthodox views about how to best practice his faith. Of his field work in England, he wrote in his journal:

> Here, in the heart and love and life of nature, and with Christ by my side, I cannot bring myself to go to church, when the whole creation calls me to worship God in such infinitely more beautiful and inspiring light and color and form and sound. Not a single thing out here

but suggests love and peace and joy and gratitude, every single thing is true, loveable, and full of virtue and praise—it is better than the best church service, there can be no doubt about it.

Wilson talked about painting, drawing and science as his way of worship. In his notebooks he wrote that his primary idea was to "make Love the ruling power of my life, the only power." And, he wrote, "Love comes to me by one channel only—the recognition of some beauty." It was through his drawings, some in the service of science, as when he was illustrating volumes on British birds and mammals, that he recognized, explored, and expressed this beauty. He wrote, "My little bird pictures are just visible proofs of my love for them, and attempts to praise God and bring others to love Him through His works."

A sermon, by Albert S. Hullah, broadcast over the BBC in London on February 5, 1928, addressed the issue of spiritual presence in Antarctica, pointing not to Wilson, but to Ernest Shackleton's mention of a divine presence during his trek across South Georgia island at the end of his famous *Endurance* journey in 1916. Shackleton wrote that during his perilous hike across the glacier-ridden terrain of the island, "it seemed to me often that we were four, not three. I said nothing to my companions on the point, but afterward Worsley said to me, 'Boss, I had a curious feeling on the march that there was another person with us.'"

For Shackleton, the veil that divided the seen from the unseen was at that moment lifted, says Hullah, making it possible for Shackleton to "see the invisible." Hullah postulated that, "There are some souls whose sense of communion with the unseen is so intimate that they feel that the removal of the thinnest veil would bring Him face to face." Maybe Shackleton was such a soul. Maybe Wilson was too. "If we put all of self into the quest, we shall become as sure of the Presence as we are of our own existence," Hullah believed. In other words, we will become as sure of what is unseen as we are of what is seen, we will become as sure of faith and imagination as we are of experience, we will become as sure of art as we are of science.

# BLACK ISLAND

B lack Island, a twenty-minute helicopter ride from McMurdo, due south across the Ross Ice Shelf, was hemmed in on one side by "dirty ice." It looked pretty from the air—pockets of turquoise amid brown, frozen rivers and pots of blue where the ice had melted and then frozen again, in what looked like patches of sand. But, I learned from Beez Bonner, the pilot flying me over, the patches of sand and blue valleys were hills and dales thirty feet high and deep. I felt as I did when I was a child, imagining myself being shrunk down to walk among stalks of grass that would tower over my head. How hard it was to know anything, to have accurate perception, when you looked down like this from above.

At Black Island the helicopter landed on an eight-foot-square pad, at first hovering uncertainly in a building wind. We were greeted by Tony Marchetti driving a yellow front-end loader. Kim Wolfe, a tall, freckle-faced, red-haired woman who was Black Island's cook, had flown over with me, and while the wind blew, we unloaded what we'd brought, tossing it all into the gaping bucket of the loader: bags of gear, boxes of cake mix, cases of beer. An especially precious box containing a pineapple, a bundle of green grapes, and some bananas was immediately run inside to the warmth of the building. Soon the flying machine and its pilot were gone, trying to beat the oncoming storm, and there were three of us left—me and two strangers with whom I wound up sharing more than a week on this volcanic hump. The storm that was nearly upon us would delay by five days the truck that was meant to take me back to McMurdo.

Tony had a mustache that looked like two rusted Brillo pads stuck to his lip, and a long, thin, blondish brown ponytail. He was bald on top. He joked that one of these days he would drag all of his hair over the naked top of his head and dress in plaid polyester pants and a white belt. It would suit him. He smoked in the back room, where all the computers were. He stayed up late listening to Jimmy Hendrix and Bob Dylan and drinking Scotch. In the morning he would sip beer with his breakfast to bring himself back to life. He was suffering from a broken heart.

Kim was just off a stint cooking for scientific parties in field camps in the high Arctic. She showed me her pictures of that adventure in Greenland, all the perfect Danish-style villages perched on the grassy edges of land with icebergs floating by. Jolly groups of vagabond scientists and their support crews in Arctic sunshine smoked cigars on the porch of a makeshift sauna. She grew up in a Wisconsin ghetto, she said, and a program she called "Hoods in the Woods" had changed her life by introducing her to the wild. She, too, was suffering from a broken heart.

Kim and Tony had made a seasonal home at Black Island for years, migrating back to this spot at the bottom of the world each Antarctic summer. You wouldn't call them friends exactly, but maybe fellow misfits who'd grown fond of each other, who'd bonded one day down at the Black Island pond marveling over the trapped bubbles of air in the ice, two people who understood each other, who'd shared with each other the most intimate parts of their lives.

The first story Tony told me was of going with Kim down to the pond and of seeing worlds, tiny air bubbles, like planets frozen in the water. He moved his hands up and up in a staggered fashion, showing me how the bubbles, layered and marvelous, were frozen in their rise. This was a significant moment to him—Kim and Tony, down at the pond, on their knees on the ice, together. She'd shown him something important to her, something small and miraculous, and he understood.

The first story Kim told me was the same story. She and I had walked down a bulldozed road to the pond, crunching in the soft volcanic soil, fighting the wind. She'd wanted to show me the island's emergency food cache, a once neatly carved mine shaft in the ice that was now a caved-in pile of snow. Kim rummaged in the mess awhile and came up with a package of frozen peas. At the pond we got down on our knees on the ice, peering into the blue clearness of it. I marveled, as Tony had, at the tiny frozen air-bubble worlds of bright white, under the glass/ice. Snow blew over the surface in long feathery fingers and the stormy sky was ten different shades of white and nearly imperceptible blue. This was where she and Tony bonded, Kim told me. She'd coaxed him into kneeling on the ice with her, just as she'd coaxed me.

From the outside, the main building at Black Island looked like a large insulated meat locker, sitting low and cheap on the rocky soil. The outbuildings looked like the metal containers you see stacked aboard barges, or piled in weedy industrial storage lots. Inside the main building were the rooms that constituted the working space and home of the two to three Black Island regulars and anyone else who stopped by to pick up or drop off a load, or fix a piece of machinery.

The most important room was the computer room, lined with red-, yellow-, and green-lit humming machines that document wind speed and other weather-related matters, as well as relay communications from Black Island's satellite dish across the frozen sea to McMurdo and back again. Black Island lies in a "quiet zone," away from the electronic interruptions of McMurdo and free from the disruptive, signal-blocking presence of towering Mount Erebus. It is, therefore, a perfect location for an enormous satellite dish that relays communications from Antarctica to the rest of the world and around again. Black Island's satellite dish takes information from the RADARSAT dome in McMurdo and sends it to White Sands, New Mexico. The RADARSAT dome collects satellite images of the whole of the Antarctic continent, which are then shared with the world in the effort to predict weather on planet Earth, among other things.

Without Black Island I wouldn't have been able to see broadcasts of the funerals of Mother Teresa and Britain's Princess Diana. Without Black Island there would have been no televised sports, no up-to-date news. It was warm in the computer room, tight with machinery, stale with smoke from Tony's cigarettes. There was a phone, a small chair, and a table.

The kitchen and living room made up the center of Black Island's living quarters. The kitchen was industrial in scale, sporting a gleaming black gas stove and oven, shining pots and pans, and wide counters. Cupboards lined the space both above the counters and below, holding mismatched bowls, cups, plates, and silverware. The table was large and topped with a pane of glass under which lay a map of the whole continent, so that at dinner a story about a particular field camp or glacier or nunatak would be interrupted by the sound of plates or silverware being moved aside so a location could be pinpointed.

Large windows in the living quarters looked out on the rock and ice of the flattened area that the whole of the tiny station sat upon, and what, in this simple landscape, seemed less like civilization than clutter—the eight-foot by eight-foot helicopter landing pad, the surrounding sheds, the satellite pad and dish covered with a giant "golf ball" that sheltered it from Black Island's fierce winds, the whirring windmills that generated the station's power, the hulking yellow bulldozer. Everything was chipped and worn by the wind, looking sanded, shredded, and beaten.

The sound of the wind was constant, both reassuring and maddening. By the second day I could see nothing out the window—nothing the third day either. Nothing most of the time. Just white whipping by, the shadows of the windmills, and the wind dancing in the sharp corners of the windowsills like white flame. For days it blew, whipped, and walloped the cluster of buildings, shook them, rattled them, and played on like thunder in our ears.

The wind blew at a hundred miles an hour, more even, only occasionally less; so fast that the windmills outside meant to harness this wind for energy slowed and then stopped, overwhelmed. The wind, said Tony, was supposed to help you sleep soundly, dreamlessly. I called Ruth from the telephone in the back room and she said that McMurdo was under siege—in the middle of a "Herbie," a Condition I, the worst kind of storm. It had roared in from the south and slammed into McMurdo. All over town ropes had been strung to get people safely from their dorms to the galley. Barrels, boxes, trash, pieces of equipment, rolled around in the wind unseen, detectable only by their rumbles and crashes.

After four days of wind, I lay in my sleeping bag and cried. The relentless wind went right to the exhausted core of me, entered me, swirled around my heart. Flapping canvas, the thud of wind on metal. Drumbeat. Heartbeat. I curled in my dreary bunk bed with the wind pulsing at the windows. I cried because of the wind, and I cried because I'd fallen deeply in love with Ruth. What was stopping me from fully embracing this new love was simple—I didn't trust myself not to screw it all up, as I had before, when I'd let myself become enslaved by others' ideas of what they wanted me to be, enslaved by my own lack of confidence, enslaved by old habits that kept the doors to my heart tightly guarded.

In those other relationships, I was like the captive maiden in the tale of Bluebeard who agrees to live on in fear, not opening the forbidden door to the chamber where her master has entombed his former wives. She agrees, in a sense, not to look the truth in the eye. Bluebeard himself is a symbol of that part in all of us that keeps us afraid and ignorant, always running away from the truth, from intimacy, from love, and therefore always captive. Love asks us to open the door and look at what's there, no matter what. This is what I had to do, I felt, before I could be a true lover with Ruth.

One night at Black Island, Kim, Tony, and I shared a spaghetti dinner with garlic bread and a rich oniony sauce. We sat around the table talking, bottles of wine emerging from shelves, bags, and back rooms. It was Tony who started it, by saying—not to us but to the table littered with cups and saucy plates and orange rind and purple-and-gold chocolate wrappers—that men are more sensitive and emotional than women. It is men, not women, who care more and talk more about matters of the heart. He showed us pictures of his girlfriend and his daughter, his home back in Driggs, Idaho, high western prairie stretching out beyond the modest country-suburban ranch houses. Lucianno Pavarotti was on the stereo, turned up high so we could hear him above the wind. Over the taut vibrations of the tenor's rising voice, Tony joked, gesturing with his head toward the source of the music—"This place is up-a-town. Little do they know we're stylin' out here." He was convinced, he said, that it was women who had harder hearts, who cared less, that it was men who were the truly sensitive ones in our culture. He produced more pictures, these of Floyd, a dog in New Zealand whom Tony frequently visited and with whom he had a loving relationship.

For a moment, Kim and Tony argued about who had more ice time—who'd spent more time in Antarctica—he or she. Their voices were taken up and mixed with the wind, the Italian singing, and it seemed for a moment I was watching them from very far away, as if they and this place were part of an old story.

"*I'm* the big banana," Kim said.

"You're the big *Antarctic* banana," Tony replied, a joke that got its power from the sorry excuses for bananas that showed up in McMurdo, bruised and frostbitten after a half-day ride in a C-130, the military cargo plane with skis that delivered supplies and people in Antarctica. "Actually," Tony added, "I've got bananas with more ice time than you." Laughing now, warmed up, he launched into stories about the old days. He'd been around so long he remembered vividly the days when the radical environmental group Greenpeace had been active in Antarctica. That was when he'd had a supply of single malt Glenlivit coming from a Greenpeace activist. In the name of that excellent scotch, Tony had defied the official order not to fraternize with activists. That was the end of an era, he said, the era when the U.S. Antarctic program used to send floating garbage out into the Ross Sea and blast it to smithereens. Now, he said, the U.S. stations are the cleanest, most "eco-groovy" places on the continent.

By now Tony was red-eyed and wasted. "Hey, eight winters," he said, referring to his own tenure on the ice. "How many stinking badges do you need? Hell. I'll tell you who deserves the badges—the guy who gets off the plane and looks around and says, 'There ain't *no* fucking way I'm stayin' down here,' and gets back on. He gets the badges, the T-shirts. Hell yeah! The guy who's been on the ice *five* minutes . . . that's my hero! Shack-a-bra-la-lip-lock, dude." He finished with a hand signal, his two middle fingers turned toward his palm, his thumb, index finger, and pinky sticking out. Pavarotti gave way to the jazzy blues of Nina Simone. Tony and Kim reminisced about the Heartbreak Thanksgiving on Black Island, the landmark year when they'd commiserated about spoiled love late into a drunken night.

"Why fall in love?" Tony asked. "You get your heart broken. Then you get to do it all over again. This is what happens: you meet someone, in ten days she says you're a great guy, then she finds out you pick your nose and snore. In the old days, our parents would have said, so what if he picks his nose, he's a great man, but us, we say, he picks his nose, I'm divorcing him." *Sukiyaki*, he said. He was thinking about committing *sukiyaki*.

Looking outside, I could barely see the shadows of the fuel tanks, a guy wire shuddering in the wind. It was Kim's turn. She talked about her boyfriend of eight years who just dumped her. They'd traveled the Grand Canyon together. They'd been writing a book about it. Another bottle of wine appeared on the table, as if announcing that this was to be an evening for hard revelation and this was the lubricant that would move it all along.

I said little about my own heart, nothing about Ruth. Already she seemed too precious to talk about, like unexpected treasure. Ruth and I had yet to lie naked together. Instead, we'd lain against one another fully clothed, feeling the heat of each other's body through our cotton shirts and jeans. Ruth had been so long without touch—the entire Antarctic winter—that she'd moaned with pleasure as she lay back in my arms. I'd been surprised and delighted at her lean hips, her muscled forearms and back and thighs, and the contrast of all that strength with the soft fullness of her breasts.

Once, when I was sick, she'd brought me the gift of an orange, and the peeling and eating of it had felt like making love. It was an afternoon, sometime in the first week of October, when all the fresh fruit on the base was long gone. I'd been sick in bed with "the McMurdo crud," a virulent version of the common cold mixed with flu bugs from all over the world, complete with fever, chills, hallucinations, cough, and a runny nose. McMurdo has a reputation as a petri dish for viruses, and at times during the height of the season as many as half the people at McMurdo could be sick with "the crud." Since there are no extra hands in McMurdo and everyone works six days a week, no one was encouraged to just go to bed and get over it. Instead, the doctor at the small medical center issued baggies of pills, and the scene became a version of some B-grade horror flick: greasy-haired, pale, feverish beings stumbling about, wiping their chapped noses, coughing, croaking out greetings to one another.

Things got so bad that at one point a town meeting was called to admonish everyone to Wash Their Hands.

When Ruth brought me the orange, I felt ashamed. I was wan, with gray circles under my eyes. I hadn't showered in days. I could smell in my room the sweet stink of my own fevered sweat. Here was my new beloved, a woman I wanted to impress with the radiant sensuality of my body, my strength, my physical desire—and I was sick.

There is something about such an encounter that is both deeply shaming and also powerfully freeing. In such a situation, you have two choices: you can take your shame and use it as a shield behind which you can hide from the truth of your vulnerability, or you can offer yourself up, sick as you are, and present yourself, stink and runny nose and all, as a candidate for love.

Ruth sat the end of my bed in her fleece vest and work boots, and offered me the orange, holding the bright orb in her outstretched hand. For a while I just looked at it, then took it in my own hand and held it. It was a small orange, smaller than a baseball. It fit perfectly in my palm. I wrapped my fingers around it, feeling the roundness of it. I smelled the thick acid of the dense, lightly pocked outside of it. For a long time I held it to my nose. Then I took my thumb and, curving it inward near the top, pushed hard with my thumbnail and peeled off the tiniest bit of skin.

Juice jumped into the air, as if it couldn't wait to get out, and my thumbnail was soon full of rind and my finger wet with tangy citrus oil. This was a tight little orange, so the skin came off in small bits, which I had to tug away with some effort. Piece by piece they came away, filling the room with the smell of somewhere far away. I piled the pieces of skin on top of one another, stacking them up into an orange tower in my lap. Finally, undressed of its skin, I considered the orange for a moment, deciding which end I would try to peel away first. Breaking the orange into halves, I gave one to Ruth and began spreading the other into sections. Each section of this tough, juicy little orange came away hard. Some I had to put into my mouth in twos. When I did that orange juice spilled out the side of my mouth and rolled down my chin onto my shirt. I didn't care if I made a mess. My mouth was full of juice, fresh juice, not sweet and not sour, but light on my tongue.

For so long I'd been frozen. To survive I'd played dead, but now I wanted so much to come alive. Instead of telling Kim and Tony about Ruth, though, I told them about my writing. I told them what I did, why I was here, the sorts of things I wanted to write about—what it looked like in Antarctica, who worked here, why they kept coming back, what the place meant to people, what it did to them, the truth about places like Black Island; how, in the midst of a huge world, this was a little hidden spot where people could have a small, definite purpose, a place where people could take shelter; how, though it was bitter cold here and the work was hard, people were the same here as anywhere else.

I told them that my story of Antarctica would also be the story of an inward journey and, like most stories of that nature, would include deadly pitfalls, kindly helpers, moments of doubt, meetings with forces of darkness, and, in the end, hopefully something good would come of it, who knew what. Tony changed the music and on came Roni Earl, singing from "Little Bit of Bad Lives": "I'm your everyday kind of man doing the best that I can."

When the wind dropped to eighty miles an hour, Kim and I went out in it, low to the ground, prowling. When we opened the door, we both hung on to it so it didn't get ripped away, with us riding it like a magic carpet. I crawled out on all fours, afraid the wind would pick me up and sail me away. Kim whooped and laughed. We had to bend over into the wind, or lean back into it, give ourselves fully over to it. It held us aloft, like a spell or a charm. What a wonderful thing, to be held up by the wind, like leaning into something invisible, yet solid and alive. It could have picked me up, as easily as a barrel, as easily as a tin roof, a piece of paper, a leaf, a seed pod, and sent me out over the rocks, into the canyons of dirty ice, rolling me across to McMurdo.

I lay down on the ground, my back against rock, and spread out, insulated against the cold, against the wind, against the hardness beneath me. How do you come to know place, especially a place so vast and wild as Antarctica? How do you come to know self? How do you come to know anything? How do you come to recognize the limits of your own life—that the years will end—and make the best of what you have left? How do you let go of wounds and resentments and fierce anger, not begrudgingly, but as an act of grace? When would I get there, if ever? First you show up, I thought. First you are present, then you can begin. *That,* I was trying to do. Back against rock, a handful of ancient volcanic soil in each fist. I was awake.

In the kitchen Kim was making chili and fresh rolls for the two men who'd finally arrived on the long-postponed supply mission, and who, when they departed, would take me with them back to McMurdo. They were outside now in the cold, in two enormous flatbed trucks called Deltas, with cabs the size of small cars. When they first arrived, Marty Reed, one of the drivers, clumped inside, radiating cold, and handed out packages. There was something for Kim from her new boyfriend in town, a young blond someone whom Tony teased her about—said she was robbing the cradle, which made Kim blush. And there was something for me from Ruth, a box labeled "Gretchen Legler: Black Island." Inside was a note from her, in her delicate, rounded, perfect longhand: "Yeah! The traverse is going. I'll get to see your lovely smile soon! I think of you often." The note was warm in my hands, I imagined, just written, the ink still moist, just come from her, just having been touched by her. She had found me, her love had come to me, way out here at Black Island.

Before she was assigned to Black Island, Kim had been a cook and baker at McMurdo, where, one winter, she also was in charge of the hydroponic greenhouse. She'd nurtured the cucumbers in the greenhouse until they were so thick they hung like sausages from a butcher-shop ceiling. One day, when she wanted to show a volunteer helper the orgy of greenery, she walked into the greenhouse and found it dark. It wasn't supposed to be dark in the greenhouse. There had been a power outage. She reached for a leaf in front of her, the leaf of a pepper, and it crumbled under her touch. Everything in the greenhouse had turned as thin and brittle as burnt paper. The whole greenhouse got reseeded in a matter of weeks, with everyone pitching in. It was a triumph. One hearty type of lettuce made it through that freeze. Kim let it go to seed and sent the miracle seed to a friend of hers in Fairbanks, Alaska.

Before I ever met Kim, I heard this story about her: after hours in the kitchen at McMurdo she and a friend filled one of the big mixing vats with hot water and jumped in naked—their personal hot tub. I asked her, during my stay on Black Island, "How *do* you make breakfast for a thousand people?" Well, she replied, "It's like learning to kayak on the Arkansas River, then going down the Grand Canyon. Once you get over the bigness of the waves, it's the same thing." Seriously, she added, "It's the same thing as making breakfast for four, you just do it in larger bowls . . . you do it in my hot tub!" Her face burst into a cheeky smile.

She showed me her cooking journal, the one she's kept of her professional cooking life. The latest chapter was from Greenland. On one page she'd pasted an empty packet of the yeast she used there, alongside photographs of golden loaves of bread. As she kneaded and shaped the bread before her, she told me the story of Jacob the baker, a story someone had told her about a baker who put little ideas on notes beside him as he worked. One time a note accidentally made it into a loaf of bread and the couple who ate it became enlightened, so Jacob started putting notes in his bread all the time. Kim liked this notion, that you could pass love, enlightenment, wisdom, comfort, through the bread you baked.

*Try it with me*, she said. *Take four cups of warm water. Just warm. Not hot.* She stuck her forefinger in and gazed out the window, clearly concentrating all her energy there—in the sensory details coming to her through her finger. She baked not by measuring, but by feeling, smelling, and hearing. *Put in oatmeal, sliced fruit, whatever you want. Put in a third cup of oil and a tablespoon of salt. Mix in the flour. Bread is so forgiving. It doesn't want much.*

We let the dough rise while I sat at the table, my head, covered by a towel, bent over a huge bowl, my face sweating beads of minty steam. I'd become sick out here at Black Island, croupy and hacky, my head heavy, my sinuses swollen. Kim had been nursing me—making batches of stinging ginger tea, and vaporous, minty saunas like this one. The room was thick with the heat of the bowl on the table in front of me, warm with the smell of bread, the aroma pushing out until it seemed to fill every nook and corner. Bread and mint and ginger and steam.

Kim next showed me how to knead with one hand. *Cup the dough, push it away with your palm, pull it close with your fingers. Like this.* She gently bent my palm over the dough. *Then put gifts inside—cheese, perhaps, dates, then close the seams. Let them rise again. Bake them when they feel full and alive.*

Kim gave me two boxes of the bread to take back with me; one I was to deliver to her young lover, and one was for me. I would take it to Ruth. Before I'd left for Black Island Ruth had come to me with a small tree of copper wire. She'd made it at her desk out of electrician's wire that she'd twisted and bent into a tree whose top was a spiral of gleaming coils. Later she'd brought me a candy bar from the small shop at McMurdo called the Ship's Store, the name a holdover from McMurdo's Navy days. She'd brought me that delicious orange. She wanted to bring me gifts, she said, but this being Antarctica and the shopping being limited, she had only these small things to offer.

Now I could bring *her* something, something from the hearth of Black Island—bread, fresh and harboring a gift of its own; a date, a piece of cheese, a slice of apple. I hoisted myself awkwardly up the high step into the cab of the Delta, the still-hot loaves in the box on my lap, and they filled the space with a yeasty perfume.

The big truck, its bed large enough to carry a tractor or a small house, lumbered along at ten miles an hour in the deep, soft snow. Eventually we came around the back side of Black Island and entered Herbie Alley, otherwise known as the Dead Zone or the radio "quiet zone," where, if there was trouble, it was impossible to call McMurdo for help. Before us, Black Island fanned off to the left and White Island to the right; between them a crazy, crevasse-filled path narrowed into infinity. As we drove I noticed the sensuousness of the hills around me; the way an ice fall came tumbling down between two rounded humps of snow, looking ever so much like a woman reclining, hip curved into the air.

We soon came upon something that looked like a hurricane-struck McDonald's. Marty explained that this was another Antarctic joke. The shack with the golden arches on top was next to an area marked KOA, for Kampgrounds of America, and was littered with the black flags that indicate a crevasse field. The shack with the golden arches was meant to be an emergency shelter, but, Marty said wryly, "If anyone ever really spent the night in there they'd have a hell of a night. The stovepipe is covered over. They'd end up like Admiral Byrd, who nearly asphyxiated himself at Little America." This was not a place where you'd want to be lost, wandering, in need of shelter. In fact, this would be Hell on Earth.

We arrived in McMurdo, finally, at midnight, to a blazing setting of the sun. I hopped down out of the truck, dragging my bag from its frozen place on the flatbed. I was dwarfed by the huge machinery, the top of my head, at five foot three, just reaching the top of the truck's wheel well. Marty waved, leaving me on a patch of frozen dirt in the stillness of the sleeping camp.

I stood for a moment, my bags piled around me. The boxes of bread, still a bit warm, were under my arm. If bread is a symbol of anything, I thought, it's a symbol of home, hope, renewal, and this bread I'd helped make took on its full symbolic weight. It was bread made here in Antarctica, in the company of so unlikely a duo as Kim and Tony, who'd made a home together on that rocky hump of land. I looked past McMurdo's little blue and white church, across the ice. There it was; Black Island, where sat the huge satellite dish that served as our connection to the rest of the world, the rest of the world's connection to all of us. Kim was probably now asleep in her bunk. Tony was no doubt still awake, drinking Scotch and listening to Dylan, consoling himself with thoughts of hard-hearted women. The wind no doubt swept around the whole rocky place, dancing at the windows, sculpting the snow, the ice, the rock. And upstairs, in my room, Ruth was waiting for me in my bed.

# DARK MATTER

The South Pole is a sacred destination not only for explorers of the secular kind, but also for scientists. Being, as it is, an extremely dark, cold, dry, nearly perfectly stable landmass, it is ideal both for scientists who look down into the mysteries at the heart of the earth, and for those who look upward, into the cosmos; seismographers and astronomers alike find a kind of utopia at the South Pole.

The day I went to the Pole was also the day I said goodbye to Ruth. Having finished her fourteen months of service in Antarctica, she was now on her way home. After first traveling in New Zealand and Australia, she would return to her beloved Vermont. Before her departure we'd exchanged our favorite shirts, so we could wear each other close to our skin. Hers was a faded green denim with a frayed collar and cuffs. Mine was almost identically soft and tattered, but blue. Standing face-to-face in the newly bare half of her dormitory room, we each slowly unbuttoned the shirt we had on, pulled our arms from the sleeves, and then, our breasts naked only a moment, handed them to each other and put them on, still warm from the other's body. With Ruth's shirt on, I felt wrapped in her, as close to being enveloped by her as I could get.

We stood together, each in the other's shirt, amid the hubbub of what was called the Bag Drag, in McMurdo's Movement Control Center, the place everyone gathered with their duffel bags, boxes, backpacks, and suitcases, when arriving or departing McMurdo. The space around us was a heaving sea of people and gear, and piles of standard-issue orange canvas bags. Ruth, like all the rest, was dressed in a full complement of what was called ECW (extreme cold weather) gear—parka, boots, wind pants, hat, mittens. Everyone shuffled forward slowly to be weighed, have their bags weighed, their passports checked.

Ruth and I had talked about this day, the day she'd leave Antarctica without me, but we'd made no plans to meet again. We made no promises. We'd shared something blissful, we reasoned, something that could never survive in the real world. A lot of Antarctic love affairs ended this way, I was told. They don't carry over into the world off the ice, where the details of regular life suffocate their magic. Although we *sensed* that we would meet again—in some other time and place—we were too coolly resigned to ask for assurances. For my part, all this indifference masked what I really felt—I didn't want to look desperate by insisting on a rendezvous in the real world. I didn't want to burden Ruth with a promise she might not want to keep. What if ours really was one of those love affairs that could only survive on the ice?

After seeing Ruth onto the bus that would take her and the other passengers down off Ross Island and out onto the ice, I shuffled back to my dorm room. I could picture Ruth on the ice runway, where she and the other passengers would file into the McMurdo passenger terminal, a boxy metal building on skids, and, after much waiting, would board the plane. I waited, kneeling at my window, until the plane launched itself into the sky. I waved farewell and quickly turned my attention to anything that could keep me from thinking of her leaving; I turned to packing my bag for the Pole.

The Pole had been the heart, the center, the long-sought prize of all of those early explorers. Given the current hubbub of frantic activity at the Pole, I was being allowed to go there only for a few nights. The science and building season had already been cut short by storms that prevented work on the new Pole from starting on time.

The airplane that took me on the three-hour, 500-mile flight to the Pole landed on the skiway not far from the entrance to the South Pole's famous silver geodesic dome— half of a huge silver golf ball plunked down upon the ice. Those of us disembarking reached the dome by first walking across a short expanse of ice and then heading down a steep, snowy ramp into an eerie, dark, corrugated metal tunnel that was fuzzy white on the inside with frost. In the hoary rime that coated the metal walls, someone had scratched a series of oblong faces, one after another, with rounded eyes, sharp noses, and straight mouths. As I walked down the tunnel, my heavy boots squeaking in the dry snow, I felt that I was entering another world, an underworld, watched by the frosted specters on the tunnel walls.

At the end of the tunnel I entered the cavern of the dome—like a giant cave, with a fifty-foot ceiling in which five holes had been cut to let in sunlight. Heat and moisture generated by activity in the dome rose and formed icy stalactites that hung from the rims of the skylights. Under the dome was a small village, including a rudimentary metal container made to look like a Swiss cottage. Housed inside the Swiss cottage and all the other containers were scientists' offices, dormitories, administrative offices, a volunteer fire department, a library, a lounge, a small hydroponic greenhouse, a recycling center, the galley, an exercise room, a medical facility—a whole town huddled close under the protective silver ceiling.

Along the edges of the dome, encircling the human habitations, lay piles of food—canned escargot, strawberry syrup, maraschino cherries, mustard, pink lemonade mix, Cornish game hens, cheese-cake, steak, and mincemeat. Some of the boxes were open, as if people had been foraging. The cooks in the galley at the South Pole, where I'd take my turn washing dishes later in my stay, made out of all this boxed mess the best food on the continent, I was told, no matter what I'd heard about the French at Dumont d'Urville, or the Italians at Terra Nova base, who apparently were known for their fine espresso.

My room at the South Pole was at the end of a long, thin cor-ridor, on the top floor of one of the metal containers. Small, muffled, and dark, it was like a secret clubhouse. The economical cubicle was just big enough for a bunk bed, a tiny table and chair, and a place to store clothes. Down the hall was the bathroom, with a row of sinks, and toilets and a shower stall. I left my bags in my room and was whisked away to explore the Pole.

In the so-called Quiet Sector, flagged off so no heavy equipment could bulldoze its way overhead, I was led down a square hole in the ice, into the side of which a ladder was planted. Down, down we descended, six feet, maybe, or ten or more, then walked through an icy tunnel, chopped square and trim at the sides, to a small cave in the middle of which sat, like a king on a throne or a toad on a mushroom, a seismograph, an instrument that measures the con-stant unseen movements of the earth. Altough a hugely technical instrument, in its operation it is not dissimilar from a rock on a spring with a pencil attached and a piece of paper below it. When the earth quakes, even as far away as Los Angeles, the seismograph here at the Pole records it by scribbling a jagged line on a sheet of graph paper, not just once, but again and again, as many as six times, as the wave of the quake makes its way around the globe.

Scientists used the seismograph to learn about the structure of the earth—what kinds of materials it was made of, what thicknesses, what densities. In fact, it was from a seismograph that scientists first learned that the earth had a molten core, a warm heart. The seismograph also demonstrated that the earth bulges at the equator—a bulge, like, say, a bulge in a peach—an effect caused, in part, by the pull of the moon. These bulges contribute to the ebb and flow of the earth's oceans by creating tides.

In the Dark Sector, where the astronomers work, massive, beautiful, gleaming telescopes were searching for answers to the most elemental questions: where did we come from, and where are we going? As the driest, darkest place on the planet, the South Pole is the ideal place for astronomers to do the cold, quiet work of looking deep into the skies.

There are three primary telescope projects at the Pole, the SPIREX, the AST/RO, and the COBRA. The SPIREX (South Pole Infrared Explorer) telescope detects infrared light from galaxies so far away that the light detected on earth takes millions of years to reach us, being released from these galaxies when dinosaurs roamed our planet. Just for perspective, said David "Finn" Barnaby—an astronomer who now works at Western Kentucky University—the human eye can see light only in the tiniest sliver of the electromagnetic spectrum. This sliver that the human eye can see covers a range of about half a micrometer and is referred to as "visible light." The SPIREX, with a range of 40 micrometers, can detect light from a much wider portion of the electromagnetic spectrum, most of which lies in the range that humans cannot see, but which we can feel as heat. Astronomers use this telescope to search distant galaxies for stars and pieces of matter, matter that is so far away and dim that it produces no light that humans can see. Because the matter produces heat, however, it can be detected by the infrared telescope.

What astronomers at the Pole are studying, in part, said Barnaby, is "dark matter." A spiral galaxy like ours gets its appearance from stars whirling around its center at high speeds. Barnaby asked, what keeps it together? What keeps the stars from flying away and the whole thing from falling apart? Gravity? Yes, but gravity from what? There are not enough stars and gas clouds to produce the gravity to hold it together. What holds it together is something we can't see, something scientists have called dark matter, which forms like an invisible halo around not just this galaxy, but others as well, preventing them from infinite expansion, from spinning themselves into nothingness. There are many hypotheses about what dark matter is. One is that it consists of very small stars and planets that don't produce much visible light but do produce heat. Others say it is some kind of matter unlike what we and our earth are made of, something invisible and not yet discovered. Scientists speculate that up to 90 percent of the entire mass within the viewable universe is made of this material, this stuff that is invisible to humans. This, at the least, is what astronomers hope SPIREX and other telescopes will help them learn, this one secret of the universe.

The AST/RO (Antarctic Submillimeter Telescope and Radio Observatory) telescope detects submillimeter radiation. Stars and other objects emit a wide palette of electromagnetic rays, or radiation, only a small portion of which we can see. Submillimeter radiation travels in waves of less than a millimeter in length, which puts it in the range between infrared light and radio waves. AST/RO scans the Milky Way for clouds of gas and dust that emit this radiation, searching for stellar nurseries in which stars are being born. COBRA (Cosmic Background Radiation Anistropy) searches for irregularities in cosmic microwaves, or the radiation left over from the big bang, the primal explosion that explains the creation of all matter and energy beginning about 15 billion years ago and that birthed our universe.

While they're gathering data to unveil these secrets, Barnaby said, scientists have other uses for the telescopes. He spoke enthusiastically of a string of photographs SPIREX took during its first year of operation, showing the impact the comet Shoemaker-Levy had when it smashed into the planet Jupiter. "We could see all the impacts," he said excitedly, pointing to a poster of the event—Jupiter an orange ball and the series of comet impacts a searing yellow. How brilliant the colors and how fast the shapes. My god, to see so clearly into the darkness!

Just as Ruth boarded the bus in McMurdo that would take her to the airplane and off the ice, I'd taken her hand in mine and pressed a gift into it. It was a drawing I'd made of the turquoise ice at Black Island, the ice that Kim and Tony and I had looked at, down on our knees at the pond: geometrical lines and cracks interrupted by round white bubbles, the crystal globes rising. Wrapped with the picture was an ordinary chocolate bar and a note: "Upon your departure from this vast, icy, white space, I wish you the best of everything. From our pirate days I remember you as an adventuresome and brave boy. You still are. I can see you now walking barefoot in the grass. Until we meet again in a green place . . ."

Such was our ease with each other, that we both felt we'd met before. We fantasized that our meeting was long ago, in another life, when we both had been pirates on the high seas, adventuresome and boyish, swinging from the rigging, playing with swords, Peter Pans of a sort, with the world by the tail. We felt so at ease with each other that when we slept entwined in one of our small beds at McMurdo, we slept well, woke up refreshed, and had good dreams, unlike, we both remarked, our experiences with other lovers, when we might wake up sore, more exhausted than when we'd gone to bed, as if we'd done battle in our sleep all night long. In one of our first nights together, lying in our clothes in the thin McMurdo bed, I'd awoken afraid and not knowing where I was, then quickly remembered Ruth was beside me, and looked at her, her black hair so dark against the pillow. As I gazed at her, she opened her eyes. "I dreamed that I didn't know where I was," she said. "Then I remembered I was with you and it calmed me." We'd had the same dream.

Whereas the three telescopes I'd seen in my first day at the Pole, with their bright mirrors and sparkling metal shells, their clean, impressive shapes and magnificent size, looked upward, another telescope installed at the South Pole looked equally as deeply downward. The logo for the AMANDA (Antarctic Muon and Neutrino Detector Array) project depicted a penguin with a telescope peering into the ice, trying to get a fix on that most elusive of particles, the neutrino, which scientists think might be another component of the mysterious dark matter, the unseen force that holds the universe together.

Astronomers know, said University of Wisconsin physicist Bob Morse, that starting with the big bang, the movement of the universe has been outward. How long will that go on? Will we eventually expand so much that we vanish? Some said the expansion would reach its limit and then reverse itself, that we would eventually end up in the big crunch. The key to answering these profound questions is to figure out how much matter there is in the universe. If there is enough, its own gravity will stop the expansion. But so far scientists have only detected about 1 percent of the amount of matter that would be required to halt the expansion. They think the rest is gravitational force from dark matter, but they don't know how much, or where it is, or what it's made of.

Neutrinos, "the little neutral ones," may be the key to identifying dark matter. The neutrino was "invented" by Wolfgang Pauli. It is basically an accountant's particle, Morse explained, invented to account for the missing energy in neutron beta decay. A neutron is unstable. It has a life of about a thousand seconds. It decays to a proton, an electron, and a neutrino. The neutrino carries off the missing energy created in the decay process. When Pauli discovered this particle with no charge and no mass that traveled at the speed of light, he declared that he'd created a particle that would never be detected. That was in the 1930s. In the 1950s the elusive particle was actually detected by scientist Frederick Reines, who won the Nobel Prize.

Though the neutrino is just barely a fact, said Morse, it's an intrepid messenger particle that may be able to lead scientists to the secrets of dark matter. Neutrinos are produced in neutron stars and black holes, far out in the cosmos. They make their way to Earth by passing through solid matter almost as if it wasn't there. They pass through everything. But as they pass through, they sometimes interact with matter, creating another elementary particle called the muon, and this is what the AMANDA project detects. At the South Pole, deep, sterile, cold holes are melted in the ice and strings of light-sensitive sensors are lowered into the holes and then allowed to freeze in place. As neutrinos pass through the ice, a few decay into muons, which in turn create flashes of light as they crash through the ice and are absorbed. The flashes coming up through the earth are how the sensors detect muons. Scientists hope to be able to trace the paths of the original neutrinos back to where they came from in outer space, thereby gaining a better idea of the sources of these cosmic travelers. The ultimate goal, Morse said, is a neutrino map of the universe that will allow scientists to look to the farthest distances for very high energy, violent phenomena that occur way, way out in the cosmos, at the very edges of the universe.

Because it takes light and neutrinos time to travel across vast distances, the telescopes at the Pole can see not only far into space but also backward in time; they see how the universe appeared when it was young. The light arriving today from even a nearby star may have taken thousands of years to reach Earth. With a powerful enough telescope, scientists can look billions of years backward, glimpsing bits of light that might have left a distant star even before our sun formed. I was mesmerized by the power of the telescopes, by the possibility of seeing so deeply into the unknown, of seeking meaning by seeking light, by peering out to the very farthest edge of darkness.

What had stopped me from confessing my love to Ruth, from pressing her to rendezvous again in another part of the world, was partly this: I didn't want her to see the black hole inside me. What really lay at my center was a mystery to me, but the certainty that what was at my core was, literally, shit came to me in repeated dreams in which I could not staunch the flow of rot. It overflowed toilet bowls. In one dream it came from between my legs, like acid, turning my clothing to molten shreds. Sometimes I imagined being able to let it all go, gushing like a geyser out of my open mouth. A part of me knew that if I could only let people close enough to see the mess inside me and if they weren't disgusted by it, if they didn't turn away, then they could help me heal. But in order to find the kind of love that would help me love myself, I had to first come to call myself beloved.

Early in our love affair, Ruth had a dream in which she and I were lying in a huge bed, dressed in white robes, settled back among the pillows, with light shining in upon us from long clean windows. Held tenderly by both of us was a baby. I'd wavered much about having a child of my own. Ruth said she didn't want children; she had enough nieces and nephews to love already. Who was this baby then? Was it some new, fresh life, a foundling? Or was it the symbol of some new thing that she and I could create together?

I was also terrified of Ruth's dream. I sometimes read with perverse interest the stories of beaten, neglected, and tortured children. I feared that a child put into my care would suffer, that the part of my self that had so little compassion for the softness in me would act out all kinds of horrible visions on a child. I had never hurt a child in my life, nor did I want to, but I was confused about whether these dreams of hurt children were an inescapable prediction or a reminder of my own most vulnerable times—the time of the knife at my wrist; those times as a teenager when I would bang my head against my bedroom wall. What was I murdering in my own dark dreams? What had to die to make way for this new life in Ruth's dream was my own murderousness toward myself.

As I lay in my bunk those nights at the Pole and turned off my light, planets, stars, whole galaxies emerged on the walls and ceilings of my room. I gasped with surprise the first time I saw them. Someone had pasted them there, a whole glow-in-the-dark solar system. I lay there, trying to sleep, hummed to by the rhythm of the generators that were the heart of the Pole, and listened to Ruth singing. I had a tape of her voice, her banjo, guitar, and mandolin, her friend Allison on vocals and Chris with his drums, a tape the band had made in McMurdo, months ago now. A whole lifetime ago now. I listened to the tape and sang along, and I practiced singing my own songs for Ruth; promising her my heart, promising her my adoration, promising her the most infinite patience, the tenderest love, if only we met again. It was as if in singing her praise, I was singing myself alive. I sang and sang, putting words to feeling, words to flesh, flesh into words.

When Ruth and I had said our final good-bye, I cried. "Why are you crying?" Ruth asked. I cried, I told her, because of the deep blue space between my hopes for my own life and hopes for me and her, and for the realization that I must always and only live now. Whole lives are made up of single days strung one to the other like beads, and right then was so wonderful, such a bead, such a gem. The months just gone by had been bliss. But I also yearned to jump ahead, to wish myself into the future with Ruth, beyond Antarctica. It was that tension between the bliss of the moment and the desire for it to last forever that made me cry. I asked her if living in the moment meant that I couldn't want for the future with her, and she said "I hope not!" To my talking about hopes, she said, "Maybe if we both have the same hopes then we really *are* enchanted."

Our talk of other lives, of other meetings in other times, was fantastic, unbelievable to us both. But we both sensed that something unseen had drawn us together, something neither of us could name; that some gentle but insistent and powerful element had pulled us from a distant time, a distant galaxy, into its orbit and kept us there. We *did* feel enchanted. Who knows, we could have been. Even scientists, with all their sophisticated seismographs and telescopes, aren't sure what the universe is made of, and we know even less about love, about the hidden, mute matters of the heart.

# CLIONE ANTARCTICA

As my eyes adjusted to the darkness, I could make out small animals floating and swimming in the dark water. These, I later learned, were pteropods, a kind of mollusk. There were also ctenophores and amphipods. The ctenophores glowed with an iridescent light, like crystals in a sunny window, scattering shafts of brilliant green, blue, yellow, and red. Small jellyfish undulated in front of me, their tentacles delicate white, almost invisible. All around the observation bell's windows other creatures hovered in the water, so numerous they seemed like pinpoints of light, like stars in a blue-black sky. They looked to me like angels, small and peach-colored, with translucent wings that waved rhythmically back and forth, as if they were flying, treading air/water, or conducting an underwater symphony.

I was sitting in the Observation Tube, a metal bell scientists had placed under the ice near McMurdo Station. The tube was made of thick metal and was painted blue. About a third of it sat above the ice, and the rest, about ten feet of it, went down below the ice, into the cold ocean. To get down into the tube, you climbed up on the metal above the ice, put your feet inside the tube, and climbed down using metal rungs in the side of the tube. The tube was about two and a half feet in diameter, a tight fit for some large people. At the bottom of the tube was a cramped area with a wooden floor and a small stool. There, through six long, narrow windows in the bell of the tube, you could sit and look out at the ocean from under the ice.

When I'd climbed my way down to the bell of the tube I sat down and took off my mittens and hat. I could hear the wind buffeting the surface of the ice around the top of the tube, but down where I sat it was quiet. Once my companions above slipped the wooden cover back over the top of the tube, I sat in darkness. I began to see the bottom of the sea ice above me: blooms of ice, great beautiful clusters of long, sharp crystals. The ice was white in some places, gray or blue in others. I could see near the tube the dive hole where divers entered the ice and then, partly sinking, partly swimming, made their way from life above to life below—to the ocean floor where they would collect sea creatures. Running to the bottom of the ocean from the dive hole was a white cord with checkered flags tied to it at intervals, a safety device, in case the divers lost track of their entryway back into the airy world. At one point in my stay in the observation bell, I was startled by a fish, probably about four inches long, that suddenly appeared in the window of the bell, fluttering its fins, pausing for a few moments at the level of my chin, seemingly examining me.

Being down in the Ob Tube made me think of a chapter from Thoreau's *Walden*, where he writes about fishing by moonlight on Walden Pond. Because he could see the sky in the water, it seemed to him that he was fishing doubly—in the water for real fish, which tugged at his line and would become his dinner, and in the sky, for ideas, for metaphorical fish, for food that would in some way feed his soul. Thoreau was as curious about the watery world under his boat as he was about the airy world over his head—spheres that he lived sandwiched between. "It was very queer," he mused, "especially on dark nights, when your thoughts had wandered to vast and cosmogonal themes in other spheres, to feel this faint jerk, which came to interrupt your dreams and link you to Nature again."

This traffic back and forth, between the literal and the metaphorical, had come to the front of my mind in Antarctica, working as I was with so many stories, my own—both the old ones I was trying to shed and the new ones I wanted to create—the heroic tales of the early explorers, the heart stories and inner journeys of those around me in the present, and the stories that scientists were uncovering and forming about this icy land—stories about its wild past and uncertain future, stories about global warming, the hole in the ozone, seals, krill, rocks, penguins, whales, fish, glaciers, the formation of matter, stars, black holes, and volcanoes. Which of these stories being made and told around me might be the best ones, I wondered. Which ways of thinking and knowing give us the best kind of information with which to make sense of the actual world and our true selves: the literal, or the metaphorical? Science, or art? I felt somewhat at odds with this world of fact that I found myself immersed in—my scientist friends with their microscopes, pipettes, beakers, calipers, and digital scales. Like most people who end up being writers or artists, I'd always been drawn to the metaphorical, to the poetic. It was the best way for me, as British novelist and essayist Virginia Woolf had put it, to see and make sense of the patterns behind the cotton wool of daily existence.

I thought much about all these things during the month I spent in closest possible quarters with scientists aboard the *Nathaniel B. Palmer*, the National Science Foundation's research icebreaker, in the Ross Sea. That mission, headed by Rice University professor Rob Dunbar, had been named ROAVERRS (Research on Ocean/Atmosphere Variability and Ecosystem Response in the Ross Sea). We were, indeed, roavers—we roamed, rambled, and zigzagged along the coast of south Victoria Land, pausing here and there to haul up samples of mud, water, and ocean creatures as well as stopping to collect measuring equipment that had been planted in the sea the year before.

For the first two days of the mission, the ship had been encased in ice offshore from McMurdo Station. Then, around midnight on that second day, the ship began to shake and rumble. The engines shifted and roared. I leaned eagerly over the sides as we split through the ice, great watery cracks opening up, spray and waves slushing up from the bow, blue-green froth sloshing wildly, ice breaking apart like brittle sugar candy. The sun blazed overhead. The ice scrubbed the metal hull. Below me on the ice, tiny penguins ran wildly just ahead of the ship. I could see the intricate designs of their tracks in the snow, along with dark specks of blood and feces left behind by seals. Clear of the ice, the ship was soon in open water, heading out into the Ross Sea. A weird clear light shone over everything. Snow petrels, like doves, their clean white wings starkly bright against the blue gray of the sea, swooped and dove all around us.

Most days on board I circulated among the scientists, asking questions, poking at specimens, helping where I could. I found the scientists and their culture to be as different as I imagined they found me and my writer's habits. Carrying my notebook and sketchpad, I could be found in unlikely nooks and crannies of the ship at all times of day, staring out to sea, reading or writing. I started many days by talking—coffee cup perched beside me—with Joe Eastman and Mike Lannoo. Eastman was a fish biologist from Ohio University in Athens, Lannoo a specialist in fish neurology from Ball State in Muncie, Indiana. They were, in addition to being a scientific team, also old friends. Their goal was simple: wanting to know what lived at the bottom of the Ross Sea, they were collecting specimens by trawling, dragging a huge net across the ocean floor. At least once a day the net was winched up and swung over the deck. When the bottom was opened, out would spill, like candy from a piñata, all manner of creatures: sea cucumbers, sea spiders, sponges, and fish.

When the net came up, bulging and dark, and its contents hit the deck, everyone rushed forward to sort through the pile of goo and ooze. They'd joke: "Seafood platter coming on deck . . . all you can . . . sort. Oh look, there's a bony arm poking out of it!" Eastman found gold in these hauls—a sweet diaphanous pink fish, for example, that he thought was a new species, although he knew only one man, a Russian scientist, who'd be able to tell him for sure. Also in the net were many specimens of *Cryodraco antarcticus*, or "icefish," which reminded me of a finely-tuned northern pike—spearlike, sharp, and boney.

Eastman was a pleasant man with a Groucho Marx mustache and a somewhat goofy manner. When he was out on deck he would eagerly paw through the catch, immediately putting the fish into large white buckets, then sorting them, photographing them, holding the fish in different poses, admiring them. Some days he'd almost quiver with excitement as he looked through the trawl net: "Oh, I know what that is . . . that's a . . ." Trying to write on a wet legal pad, he'd succeed only in ripping the paper.

From these trawls Lannoo would select specimens and prepare them for storage and transport, pinning them down in metal trays, surgically opening the fish and infusing their circulation systems with preserving chemicals. Lannoo was a shy, rough looking, boyish man, with huge beautiful eyes and long lashes, a scarred-over cleft in his upper lip. As he leaned against a workbench in his orange rubber coveralls, a bright light close to his specimen tray, his hands in surgical gloves, gleaming steel tools in his fingers, carefully picking at the brain tissue of a *Cryodraco antarcticus*, the sound of the sea outside, the smell of fish and fuel and salty cold water all around, we would talk.

We talked at length about his involvement with the Declining Amphibian Populations Task Force, an international group set up by conservationists to investigate population declines and deformities in frogs and other amphibians. The debates about the causes of the decline are highly politically charged, pitting those who believe parasites are the culprit against those who believe the harm is due either to UV radiation or to the use of insecticides and other human-driven causes. Whichever scientist can best "sell" his or her story garners grant money to continue research, Lannoo said. Frogs and salamanders are our canaries in the coal mine, he insisted. They are telling us something important about environmental conditions for humans. He spoke urgently and passionately, all the while delicately pinning back the flesh of the fish in front of him.

Lannoo talked admiringly of John Steinbeck's book *The Log from the Sea of Cortez*, Steinbeck's journal of his collecting trips down the Baja coast and up into the Sea of Cortez. Steinbeck's goal was to see what kinds of animals lived in that place, so that he and others might learn more about how to live in some sort of harmony with them. Lannoo gives the book to all of his graduate students to read. This was the kind of scientist he wants to encourage them to be—whole ecosystem scientists. This was the kind of scientist Eastman and Lannoo were. They were, Eastman said, what you'd call "whole organism" people, as opposed to what he called "molecular" people. Eastman and Lannoo focused their study on whole members of ecosystems, whole fish, rather than on molecules and atoms and other things that can't be seen with the naked eye. Although Eastman felt like a tweedy, bow-tied professor in the midst of a new age of molecular biology, there was still important work to be done on his end: he and Lannoo were working in a field where the big picture had yet to be discovered. "People have been coming to the Ross Sea for a hundred years and we still have things to learn about the diversity of the ecosystem here," Eastman said, excitedly.

I felt most comfortable talking with Eastman and Lannoo because I felt somehow that the process of their "old-fashioned" science was closest to my own process as a writer. I too worked with relatively unsophisticated tools—a notepad, a pen, a computer, and my own mind. I too was driven by a kind of simple wonder and curiosity. I too was surprised and excited by what came up in my net. My narrative process also was laborious, requiring as it did, much collecting, ruminating, musing, sorting, arranging. Though our processes were very alike, they also were different. In the work of the scientists on board the *Nathaniel B. Palmer*, numbers had been enshrined as the most reliable form of information about life on Earth. And what did I have in my notebooks? Not numbers. Nothing objective, certainly. I had only words. Only impressions. Only visions. Only the incomplete sense that my single, idiosyncratic mind could make of the data my body brought in: what it saw, what it heard, what it felt, what it tasted, what it smelled.

In the *Song of Solomon*, which I'd heard read on my first Sunday in Antarctica at McMurdo's Chapel of the Snows, the king tells the story of his desire for his love and her body in metaphor:

> Behold, thou art fair my love;
> behold thou art fair;
> Thine eyes are as doves behind thy veil;
> Thy hair is as a flock of goats
> That lie along the side of Mount Gilead.

> Thy teeth are like a flock of ewes that are newly shorn,
> Which are come up from the washing,
> Whereof every one hath twins
> And none is bereaved among them.

> Thy lips are like a thread of scarlet
> And thy mouth is comely.

He goes on, shameless, elaborate, outrageous even:

> Thy temples are like a piece of pomegranate . . .

Thy two breasts are like two fawns that are twins of a roe
Which feed among the lilies . . .

The hair of thine head like purple . . . the smell of thy breath
    like apples.

The joints of thy thighs are like jewels
The work of the hand of a cunning workman.

Thy navel is like a round goblet,
Wherein no mingled wine is wanting:
Thy belly is like a heap of wheat
Set about with lilies.

How else was he supposed to tell the story of the depth of his passion except to reach for metaphor—to compare his love to all the things that were to him of most value: goblets, jewels, wheat, wine, and goats?

As my scientist comrades shared their work with me, showing me queer animals from the bottom of the ocean—sea spiders, polychaete worms, krill, diatoms—I drew pictures; especially on days when words were too much to handle. I sat with watercolor pencils and pastels, trying to bring to life in color and shape what I was seeing around me. My drawings revealed coral-colored sea spiders with too many legs, purple diatoms spread across a green background like rubies in a jewelry box, a feathery gold polychaete worm on a royal blue background that could have been a kite in a dark sky.

Like Solomon's visions of his beloved, my visions of Antarctica were exaggerations; they were not accurate, by any means, but then accuracy was not my goal; interpretation was. The images I created, full of wonder and imagination, continue to move me and others to whom I show them in ways that more factual photographs of Antarctica do not. They seem still to speak with many voices—a rich babble of fact and longing.

Early in our knowing one another, I'd drawn Ruth a picture of what I'd seen through the windows of the Observation Tube and then secretly put it on the seat of her pickup truck, which was parked with the other orange trucks in the gravelly center of McMurdo, plugged into electrical outlets to keep their engines warm. I imagined her finding my drawing the next time she was called out at midnight to check a fire alarm in some remote building. The picture showed the undulating tentacles of the jellyfish, the crystalline blooms on the bottom of the ice above me, and the tiny pink beings I had no name for. As I'd drawn the picture, my sense of wonder and my growing feeling of love for her all became a part of the image that finally emerged on paper with its improbably dark and steady blue, its whimsy, its primitive lines and shapes. We called the creatures Ross Sea Music Fairies, because they looked like tiny, peach-colored symphony conductors with their tuxedo tails draped down their backs.

As I watched the dedicated, intelligent men and women aboard the *Nathaniel B. Palmer* work in their labs among all the technological paraphernalia of modern science, I wondered what was behind it all for them. Before coming into such close contact with professional scientific culture, I had my own naive versions of what motivated scientists: I used to think that scientists did what they did because they loved the world, because they felt tenderly about seals, say, or were taken by the comic beauty of chinstrap penguins; that there had been some epiphanic moment in the childhood of every successful scientist that led him or her to want to search out the secrets of the universe, to see behind the veil. I remembered vaguely a conversation I once had with my own scientist father about the value of knowledge for its own sake, a conversation in which he was on the side of knowledge and I wasn't. Even then, I couldn't imagine the value of knowing a fact without a story to put it in. Perhaps this is why I excelled at math only when I could do what were then called "story problems," where numbers were turned into piles of oranges and cups of flour.

In my mind, Scott's chief scientist, Edward Wilson, was the ideal form: he was a scientist, an artist, and a deeply spiritual man, who in his writings unselfconsciously linked all three. In a letter to his wife, Oriana, he wrote, "The more quietly and privately one lives with God's own gifts, the more one fits oneself for helping others to see them. That's the one thing I have always felt God meant me for—to show his glorious Beauty to others." In another letter to her from Antarctica he wrote: "I long to do as much as I can that others may share the joy I find in feasting my eyes on the colors of this wonderful place, and the vastness of it all." His science was motivated by love, by awe, by wonder, and by the urge to communicate that wonder to others. As a scientist, he felt it was his calling to seek new knowledge, new animals, new *beauty* and to share his discoveries through the language of science and art. I wanted to think scientists were mostly like Wilson, mostly like Mike Lannoo, who felt the disappearance of salamanders and frogs as a personal wound; mostly like Joe Eastman, who practically swooned over the beauty of fishes. I was sure that inside every scientist was a poet.

The real name of the angelic, winged creatures that had so captivated me that I'd drawn their picture for Ruth, was *Clione antarctica*. They were, I later learned, a snail-like animal whose wings were the remnant of a lost shell. The little mollusk, in fact, was the subject of study by scientists Bill Baker and Jim McClintock, who discovered that this small sea butterfly carried a chemical that repelled predators, a chemical that protected it so well that amphipods, small shrimp-like animals, actually captured the tiny things and attached them to their backs, holding them hostage in a way, so that *Clione*'s powers then protected them both.

# ANTARCTIC NAVIGATION

Aboard the *Nathaniel B. Palmer* the days became strangely blurred and the ocean became lulling and heavy. At night the ship rolled from port to starboard, tipping me in my bed, so that my head leaned downhill, the top of my skull pressing against the wall behind my pillow. Sleep was barely possible, unused as I was to the movements of the sea. The ship carved through three-foot-thick ice pack, then would stop, back up, and ram the ice again. When the bow pried into the ice, the whole ship trembled, shuddered, stuttered, creaked, and groaned. The vibrations traveled up through the metal hull, through wood, through carpet, through my mattress, and entered my body, which vibrated with the rumble.

When the rolling, the crunching, the stultifying smell of diesel fuel, and my own fidgety mood became too much, I went on deck and watched from above as the ship plowed through the ice, keeping a steady forward course toward the next station, where we would stop again and the ROAVERRS scientists would lower their instruments over the side to collect water, mud, fish, and other sea creatures. On deck, as I looked over the side of the ship, down the long orange metal hull, I could see the ice peeling away; it would rise in great broken slabs, its bottom pearly green and sometimes flecked with rusty-brown algae, then it would fall back, bobbing up and down in the gray-blue water, piling upon itself. As we moved through the ice, the ship stirred up krill and petrels followed, swooping and gliding in our wake.

I stood for hours at the rails of the ship, sweeping my eyes across the iceberg-studded water. Some bergs had been carved into ragged mountains by the wind and water. Others had been hollowed out, into floating blue caves. The light played upon the ice, painting the bergs electric blue, jade green, yellow, pink, and orange. On some days I could see far off the coast of Victoria Land and the great towering edge of the continent, or we might cruise by an island, dark and topped with brilliant snow, like a frosted plum pudding. Often I could see penguins and seals resting on flat bergs. Stormy, gray, fog-beshrouded days alternated with days of blinding sun, blue skies, and blood-red sunsets.

After prowling the lower decks I often would walk up to the bridge to get a view of the ice from sixty feet high. Sometimes the ship would leave the ice altogether, entering a polynya, an ice-free spot of water within a larger ice pack, where the water was flat calm. One day when the water was still as pudding, calm and silent, I heard a splash, and looked down from the bridge to see ever-widening circles in the dark water. Three penguins rose up, like dolphins. They leapt and dived and swam under the water; their wings, which on land seemed so useless, worked like any bird's wings, allowing them to fly with grace through the sea.

I developed my own rhythm on board the ship. Each day after waking I would take coffee, an orange, and crackers to the back deck, where I would lean against a pile of fishing net, or sit on an upturned crate, feeling wind on my face, feeling the cold, and smelling the sharp scents of ocean brine and ship fuel. I would drink and eat there, then travel up each level of deck, pausing as I went to observe, to take notes, to mark the weather, to record the icy, watery landscape, eventually ending up on the bridge. There I would meet with Troy Endicott, the third mate, who walked me through the most elementary rules of Antarctic navigation.

Endicott was patient, perhaps even amused, and each time I entered the bridge he would move in anticipation toward the console where the charts were spread. I hovered over the charts, asking him to help me pinpoint our location. Where were we, I wanted to know. Where was I, exactly? The exercise was in the end futile: what did it matter where I was, or where the ship was? It mattered to Endicott because he had to keep the ship from crashing into an island. It mattered to the scientists because they had to get to their next multimillion-dollar mooring and collect its precious data. Yet, for me, location was inexplicably bound with feeling and little else. On some days, the feeling of being in limbo was excruciating.

In my time on the bridge, hovering over the charts, gazing out the expansive windows, I often got to see the captain, Joe Borkowsi. He'd been a ship's captain for nearly twenty-five years and had been sailing in Antarctic waters since 1992. His Cajun accent turned *Ant-arc-ti-ca*, a four-syllable word full of hard consonants, into the rolling, smoothly delivered *Annahdika*. His home was Morgan City in the "Great State of Louisiana." He said *riva* for river, *oistahs* for oysters, *hea* for here. He was dark, round, and beefy, and wore gold chains and a gold earring in his left ear, which made him look somewhat piratical. Like all good captains, I imagine, Borkowski was sentimental about his ship. That year, as in other years, the *Nathaniel B. Palmer* had set out from Chile and was required to cross the Drake Passage, which the captain confirmed was the roughest sea in the world, keeping all but "the biggest boys" out of the water. This ship and this crew had been all over the world, the captain said. He glanced quickly about, seeming the smallest bit self-conscious about waxing so, but, seeing no sign of teasing, continued: "We *love* this ship. I can speak for all of us, for the crew, for Marta and the galley, *all of us*. We love this ship."

I borrowed from the captain a three-ring binder labeled *The Ice Book*. Printed on the cover was: "Maiden Voyage of the *Nathaniel B. Palmer*. Ice Navigation and Ice Seamanship. Capt. Ewald Brune." Brune was the ship's ice pilot on its maiden voyage in 1992. Most of the book's contents was written in an elegant longhand. On the first page—written in careful pencil in large letters, as if Captain Brune wanted to drive home this one point above all, as if he really wanted his readers to learn one thing—was this: "Never forget. The ice is telling you what to do and not you are telling the ice what to do." I read through the book, settled in one of the comfortable up-holstered high chairs set back from the navigation console on the bridge. From where I was I could see where the ship was headed and had full view of either port or starboard side, depending on which side of the bridge I'd chosen to sit on that day. The landscape was comfortingly similar on most days—shades of gray, white, and black. Some days the ship would move close to the land, face-to-face with the lolling tongue of a glacier; or it would sidle up to the towering icy edge of the continent; or cruise near a dark, snowcapped island; or push through water crowded with massive violet bergs or plates of thin pancake ice.

One day we spent time up against the Great Barrier, as Scott called it, the edge of the Ross Ice Shelf—the barrier to the conti-nent, to the South Pole, to the heart of this icy land. The captain had pulled the ship close, within touching distance it seemed, of the hundred-foot-high frozen edge. We stayed there for more than an hour, all of us leaning over the bow, reverently silent or whispering if we talked at all. In either direction, as far as any of us could see, the wall of ice ran, vanishing into infinity, high and perfectly carved of white and shades of blue, lavender, and turquoise, flat on top and rising eerily straight. I admired the shapes in the wall, the cracks and crevasses and the deepening blues and purples, the turquoise where the ice met the water. If I could climb up on top of that wall of ice, I thought, I could walk all the way to the Pole. Some crazy, love-fired desire to test myself, to raise my own expedition and head out, burned in me. I would leap off the bow now, swim to the wall, scale it and run all out for the center! Nearby, whales blew plumes of spray into the air, their black backs just rising out of the water. As we moved closer, Captain Joe blew the ship's horn, *booooooooom!* The sound bounced and hollered up and down the blue-white wall, and came rushing back into our ears.

Near midnight on Christmas Eve, I heard what I thought was a tape of the Chipmunks singing Christmas carols, but upon further investigation, ducking my head into one of the ship laboratories, it turned out to be Harry, one of the young scientists, playing Beatles songs on his guitar. He cradled the small guitar next to his chest and sang in a high-pitched, thin voice, "Picture yourself on a boat in Antarctica with pe-e-en-guins and strawberry bergs. . . ."

On Christmas morning we assembled in the galley, where imaginative renditions of Christmas stockings had been hung along one wall, and the tables had been decked with small plastic trees and candy canes. Jenny Fox, a computer assistant, had made a stocking from two paper printouts of a satellite image cut in the shape of socks and stapled together, with the words, "Santa We Are Here," written on it and a big red arrow pointing to our exact location. The captain parked the ship securely in a stretch of frozen sea. The barbecue, a metal drum on legs, was lowered over the side, the gangplank was put down, and we trailed out onto the ice to stand in loose groups, to throw snowballs, and to chase each other in the crusty snow while holiday music came floating out to us from the ship's speakers. Steaks, hamburgers, and sausages were roasted on the grill. Inside, Marta and the other cooks in the galley prepared pecan pies, cookies, chocolate candies, sweet breads, and salads.

Outside, crew and scientists wandered in an amazed stupor amid the penguins, who came up to us in groups of three, six, ten, to investigate. Pictures were taken. I imagined then that the scenes to emerge on film would be much like those I'd seen of Robert Falcon Scott's or Ernest Shackleton's expedition members playing football on the ice—thin dark figures frozen in action, leaping, catching, tumbling, running, against a background of nothing. The whole of the scientific crew aboard the vessel posed in the bright glare beneath the ship's massive orange prow, the magnitude of it dwarfing us all. The incongruity of that huge ship, the smoking barbecue out there on the ice, the crew grilling burgers and steaks, the tiny Adélie penguins, and us, all amid the extreme flatness was so bizarre, so otherworldly, that it was hard to reconcile.

After the festivities, when the gangplank had been drawn up, the barbecue hoisted back on board, when the ship shuddered and moaned and then broke free of the ice to be once again on its way, I traveled along the outside decks up to the bridge again, where I listened with much interest to holiday radio chatter from McMurdo and remote field camps. The sounds came and went, breaking off, fading out, then blaring back amid crackling static—voices celebrating a holiday in this vast, wild place; human beings connecting themselves to one another via ephemeral radio links. People were playing Christmas songs for one another on harmonicas and guitars. There was laughter and the unmistakable sound of drunkenness. After a harmonica rendition of "Jingle Bells," someone said, "Thanks buddy, that was awesome . . . Have one for me, over . . . Roger that, buddy . . . Pyramid out . . . Andy clear." It was easy banter between longtime colleagues and friends. Or perhaps new friends that life in Antarctica had made intimate, generous, and kind more quickly than if any of these radio talkers had met in the context of their real lives. More off-key singing and laughter came from the radio: "Joy to the world. Hen-ry has come. The Twi-in Ot-ter is here." Someone was celebrating the arrival of a small airplane at their field camp. There was the sound of applause. "Brilliant, brilliant, encore, encore . . . Merry Christmas, that'll be Mac Ops clear." It struck me to be happy about all of it, all this gratuitous chatter; happy that these were all voluntary gestures, meant in good humor and kindness, and received well, a triumph over forces that would have us, any of us, disconnect from ourselves or one another, sign off, as it were, let the radio go dead. Instead of distance, instead of isolation, this landscape, this Antarctica, inspired closeness.

Some days the horizon burned gold and blue and the wide sky was scattered with snow petrels, and on those days the simple clarity of the sea and the sky surrounded me as I settled in with the captain's *Ice Book*. I plodded through basic information about ice: fresh water freezes at 32°F; seawater freezes at 28.6°F. The most important characteristics of ice are salinity, density, and strength. Sea ice is divided into four categories—new, young, first year, and old. I scanned diagrams that showed how to move ships around various kinds of bergs; included was the warning, "Give all icebergs a WIDE BERTH." Chapter headings included "Antarctic Navigation," "Beset in Ice," "Celestial Navigation," and "Dead Reckoning."

I read on: "Much literature has been written with respect to the inferiority and/or lack of charts in Antarctica which can be summarized as the following concerns: lack of detail, inaccuracy, coverage." To illustrate this point further, Captain Joe told a story: The ship was headed to Chile's Antarctic base, on the Antarctic Peninsula. "We were going at zero visibility, we were goin' on *chawts*, and *chawts* down hear ain't worth"—he paused for effect—"shit. What we thought was icebergs was islands and what we thought was islands was icebergs and we were in fast ice." He moved his hand, upright, like a ship moving through the ice. "Suddenly we saw this little light. So we stopped. When it cleared"—he looked around and moved his hands in a clearing motion—"the station is RIGHT there." He stepped forward, jabbed his index finger sharply, and bent his neck as if he was looking down off the bridge to something small directly below him. "The Chileans said, 'We *neva* seen someone come between those islands like that. We *neva* seen someone so close to the station."' He laughed and whooped, "Lord have mercy!" Everything is challenging in *Annahdika,* said the captain, especially the ice and the uncharted waters. "We're always redrawin' our *chawts,*" he said. "We're always redrawin' our *chawts.*"

I had become obsessed, in Antarctica, with maps, directions, locations, compasses—anything that would help me see, in a larger context, where I was. One day in McMurdo, I took lessons from Royal, aka "Buck" Tilley in how to use a GPS, or Global Positioning System. Besides being the "sea ice mapper" at McMurdo, Tilley was a teacher at McMurdo's "ice school" and "snow school," both required for anyone leaving McMurdo Station for day trips or longer stays at field camps. His lessons were always full of wry humor: "When you go out in the field, take everything with you. That way you can shiver inside your sleeping bag." He would open a big orange bag—a survival bag—meant to include everything a person would need if stranded on the ice. "What's this?" He held out an ice saw. "The world's biggest bread knife!" In Antarctica, he said, clothes should be as unfashionable as possible.

Knowing how to use a GPS is necessary in Antarctica because, as Captain Joe had made so clear, charts are unreliable, and compasses are virtually worthless. A GPS is a handheld device, the magical powers of which are based on twenty-four satellites that circle the earth 11,000 miles up every twelve hours. The GPS works on the ancient principle of triangulation. You need at least three of the circling satellites to verify your location. The device measures the distance between where you are (the place from where your GPS is sending its signal) to the satellites, based on the travel time of radio waves, which travel at the same speed as light—186,000 miles per second. The satellites have fixed locations in space, just as the stars or the sun did for the ancients, so once you know the travel times of the radio waves between your location and various satellites, you can plot your location.

During our lesson at McMurdo, Buck handed me the GPS, turned it on, and it came to life in my hand, its small green-yellow screen filling up with a circle surrounded by small squares. This was called "acquiring." The small squares on the screen were satellites. Buck said, "If you turn this on and set it out somewhere under a big open sky and wait ten minutes, it will know where it is on the planet." He cautioned me, however, against thinking it was a perfectly reliable navigational device. For instance, he said, "You can't walk a tightrope with a GPS. It has a built-in inaccuracy of 150 feet."

We drove around McMurdo in a pickup truck, me punching in coordinates as we stopped at various locations. In this way, I created a route, filing it in the GPS's memory. Charting a route in such a way might save the life of a scientist trying to make her way back to McMurdo in the midst of a storm—leading her along a path to safety. When Buck and I came around our course the second time, we had a map to follow, a map that manifested itself as a little road on the screen of the GPS. "See that diamond?" Buck asked, pointing to the screen in my hand. "That's us. See that line? That's what we want to drive on. If we go over here"—he turned the truck slightly off the real road and we swerved madly off the path on the screen— "Aieeee! We're in a crevasse!" he screamed in mock horror.

As we made our way along, another beat-up orange pickup inched toward us on the road. I imagined two beat-up pickup trucks meeting on a dirt road running between farms in southern Minnesota. Buck rolled down his window. The man in the other truck, Bill Haals, the seasonal operations manager for McMurdo, was wearing a baseball cap and a grin. He rolled down his window, and they leaned out to talk.

Bill: "Whatcha doin?"

Buck: "We're trying to figure our where the hell we are."

Bill: "Billings, Montana."

Buck: "No!"

Bill: "Well, they flew you around in a windowless aircraft awhile. You could be anywhere."

We drove on, stopping again outside the Movement Control Center. This was where you went to catch a ride out of McMurdo to the South Pole, to Siple Dome or other field camps elsewhere on the continent, to New Zealand, to home. This was also the site of the post office. I hit "Mark" and "Save" and the GPS told me exactly where I was: south 77 degrees, 50 minutes, and .825 second; east 166 degrees, 41 minutes, and .099 second.

Each day aboard the *Nathaniel B. Palmer* I would mark our locations using my GPS, keeping close track of where we were on larger maps in the science labs and on Endicott's charts. As I passed the time, I scoured the map of Antarctica—the huge lobe of the eastern part, the smaller lobe of the West Antarctic Ice Sheet, and the continent's ragged horn pointing toward South America, looking it over hungrily, greedily, with much fascination, marveling at the pinprick of McMurdo Station in the vast expanse, marveling at the wonderful names of things. All around the edge of the continent were the stations of various nations: Terra Nova Bay belonged to Italy; Gondwana to Germany; Leningradskaya to Russia; Commonwealth Bay to Australia; Dumont d'Urville to France; Zhongshan to China; Syowa to Japan; Dakshin Gangotri to India; Sanae to South Africa; Jutulsessen to Norway; Aboa to Finland; Svea to Sweden. The great white interior had only two stations, the United States' Amundsen-Scott South Pole Station and the Russian station at Vostok.

After noticing the names of all the stations, my eyes would roam further: there was the Ingrid Christensen Coast, Queen Mary Coast, Sabrina Coast, Adelie Coast, Wilkes Land, Queen Maud Land, Marie Byrd Land, Cape Russell, Cape Sibbald, Cape Goodenough, Farewell Island, Tucker Inlet, Pryor Glacier, Moscow University Ice Shelf, Bay of Winds, Windless Bight, Goodspeed Nunataks, Dismal Mountains, Cape Longing, Moody Point, Danger Island, the Geologists Range, the Queen Elizabeth Range, the Royal Society Range.

I found on the map of this immense continent, features that bore the name of my beloved. There was Mount Ruth, at 86 degrees and 18 minutes south, 151 degrees 45 minutes west, near the Bartless Glacier in the Queen Maud Mountains; a ridge-shaped mountain, it was named by Richard Byrd for the deceased wife of one of his expedition members. There was Ruth Ridge, at 64 degrees 39 minutes south, 60 degrees 48 minutes west, near the Detroit Plateau on the east coast of Graham Land. Dr. Otto Nordenskjold named this black, rocky ridge after his sister. Antarctica is a continent of beautiful names.

Like Captain Joe, I was having to redraw my chart. And why not? The odds against meeting Ruth at all had been so great, the relief at my adoration of her and her welcoming of it so profound. It was as if we'd both been rescued, hauled up from a foaming, disturbed ocean and flung, panting, onto an ice floe of our own, side by side. It seemed so simple now: Ruth was willing to be adored by me and eager to offer me adoration in return. We were both hungry to give love, ready to lavish upon each other what we hadn't been able to spend in the past. And we were both shocked, startled, at the joyous ease of the exchange.

Ewald Brune's advice about ice—"Never forget, the ice is telling you what to do"—was beginning to penetrate. *Wake up*, some voice was hollering inside me. *She is the gift you've been looking for for so long. Do something.* The ice is the immovable, natural thing, the thing that you work around, Brune had written. Like instinct. Like feeling. You can't ignore it, or force it, or tell it what to do. Instead, you obey it.

I went to work to find her.

Ruth had told me she might stay at a women's guesthouse in Christchurch. I used the sea phone in a tiny closet-size office onboard the ship to call her, waiting each time I called until satellites lined up in just the right way with the direction of the ship at precisely the right time of day. I made the same call so many times the proprietess came to recognize my voice. Then one day, Ruth arrived. When she came to the phone, I yelled into the receiver, trying to out shout the static, and talked fast, hoping to say what I had to say before the line went dead. I stood in the middle of that tiny office, my legs braced against the roll of the ship, staring out the oval porthole at the heaving gray ocean, ice, and sky. "There's something important I have to ask you," I yelled, and before I'd even finished, she replied: *Yes. Yes,* she said. *Yes. Yes.*

Afterward I went directly to a map. I wanted to know exactly where the ship and I had been at 6:06 Greenwich mean time on that perfect day. "What happened there?" Dunbar asked me, as he watched me tracing the lines of latitude and longitude. He peered closer to see the spot my finger had pinpointed. "What happened at 75.5 south, 168 east?" he asked.

"Something wonderful," I said.

# A MAP OF THE HEART

W hen the *Nathaniel B. Palmer* docks at McMurdo's pier, I am asleep. Hours later, my body sensing that the ship is no longer moving, I wake up with a start, banging my head against the top bunk.

Scott's low wooden Discovery hut appears outside my porthole window, dusted with snow. Scott's ship, which rested here nearly a hundred years ago, would have been all wood and mast and sails. In contrast, our ship is an orange metal monster that dwarfs Scott's hut. We are finally still—the ship, the hut, the land around it, also still, brown and black, so unlike the sea we've come from.

Up the hill from the pier are McMurdo's familiar brown dormitories, its fuel tanks and its tiny blue and white chapel. Faces peer down at us from the dormitory windows. People wave. The gangplank is down. There are stirrings on deck. Outside snow is swirling and it is minus six degrees. Orange pickup trucks are now arriving to collect cargo, and all is busy on deck. Snow is falling more heavily, the sky is white. We are here!

There's a flight leaving for New Zealand the next day, I'm told, and I'm scheduled to be on it. I'm nearly sick with excitement. I'd girded myself to spend at least two days, maybe three, in McMurdo, but when I learn that I'm twenty-four hours closer to being with Ruth, all patience and calm dissolve. I'm so eager to meet Ruth in New Zealand that I pack my duffel bag in minutes and run down the gangplank and up the hill to "bag drag." Since I have but one more night to stay in Antarctica, I'm housed in Hotel California, named, in jest, after the song by the Eagles that contains the ominous line, "You can checkout any time you like / But you can never leave." In this McMurdo dormitory those who are ready to leave but haven't yet left bide their time. We're called the "ungone."

In my last afternoon I wander around McMurdo. I amble down to Hut Point, up the hill to the statue of the Virgin Mary that overlooks the bay. I pick up my boxes at the post office and share their contents—chocolate, salami, gourmet cheeses—with friends at a picnic on the floor of one of the laboratories, among the pipettes and beakers. We make toasts, to Antarctica, to love, and to leaving. That night I cannot sleep for excitement.

The next morning, early, I call the Movement Control Center and the woman who answers says, "Have you had your coffee yet?

"Not yet," I reply, startled. My stomach does a small flip.

"Why do I have to be the one to deliver bad news?" she asks.

I am, against my will, starting to cry. I tell her I won't take it personally and I won't hold her responsible. She should just tell me the truth.

"A twenty-four hour delay," she says, and I hang up the phone.

I can't eat. I don't want to talk to anyone. But Charlotte, aka "Huck," later drags me to lunch, where I peel the skins off grapes and pick out the seeds. I wander around McMurdo—to the hydroponic greenhouse, where, I reason, at least the green plants and sweet humidity will cheer me up.

I remind myself that it's like this all the time in Antarctica. In fact, it could be worse. Months earlier, in November, air traffic was so snarled at McMurdo and the place was haunted by so many of the "ungone" that it seemed like a zombie movie. Full, thick, roiling white fog crept in each night and hunkered over the town most of the day. No supplies came from New Zealand. There was no fresh food for Thanksgiving.

I prowled around with my reporter's notebook, searching for explanations for the delays. I went to the weatherman. The worst in nine years, he said. High pressure, low pressure, cooling air, dense fog. Nothing to push it out of the way. The manager of flight operations spoke in terms of "goes" and "no goes." The flight board was a mess all through November. Virtually no mail arrived the whole month. The wall calendar inside the post office was marked daily: Scratch. Negative. Zero. Squat. Nechevo. Nyet. Zippo. Zilch. Nun. None. Nada. Nope. Diddly. Goose egg. Naught. Every morning hopes would rise, as scientists and support workers anticipated their departure, only to be dashed once again when the plane from "Cheech," a nickname for Christchurch, turned around at the Point of Safe Return, or the planes at McMurdo were unable to depart. Weather, mechanical problems, tired pilots—it was a different story every day, but it didn't really matter.

November, that month of so much consternation and so many cancelled flights, the month of my birthday, was also the month I took the "Polar Plunge" in one of the science dive huts at Hutton Cliffs, not far from McMurdo. Inside the orange and green dive shanties, in addition to a kerosene heater, a cookstove for preparing warm drinks, a stash of high calorie food, and a wooden counter, there was a plywood floor with a four-foot-square hole cut in the bottom. Inside this wooden square was the round, icy doorway into the ocean.

When the divers and I entered the hut that day, a female seal and her baby occupied the blue hole in the floor, curved around each other like yin and yang, the complementary halves of Chinese cosmology. The mother was large and silvery black with wetness and light. Enormous whiskers sprayed out from her face, her dark eyes mirroring us back to ourselves. She was my size, I figured, about five feet long. Her whiskered, big-eyed child floated fearlessly next to her. After some moments of attention from us, they deftly turned and disappeared into the sea, into that long green and white tube that led from the plywood floor of the hut down into that other world.

I'd gone with the divers before, helped them don their diving suits, helped them pull on their cumbersome, insulated rubber gloves, their masks and rubber hoods. I'd waited for them, done the things a dive tender does. I made cocoa for when they came up in a whirlwind of bubbles, up out of the blue in their red and yellow suits. I cranked up the heater to high. When the divers came up, their faces blue and immobile, ice on their regulators, their lips puckered with cold, they'd slip out of their tanks and weight belts in the water, handing them up to me to place on the wooden floor. Then they'd hoist themselves up to sit on the edge of the hole. They'd pull up their specimen bags and show me leggy sea spiders, urchins, and creatures that looked to me like delicate wine-colored flowers. They'd tell me stories about baby seals chasing them, nipping at their flippers. They'd say that once they were down there it was so beautiful they'd forget about the cold.

While I waited to do the "Plunge" that day, I wandered outside the dive hut. The blowing snow shifted and cleared, alternately concealing and revealing the seals that lay atop the ice. They looked to me like cattle lying on an icy, windswept pasture, their great bulk hunkered down benignly on the white flatness. There were so many of them, maybe forty, some disguised as mere hummocks. They bellowed and barked, drummed and thumped. Their sounds were melodious and ridiculous, musical and disgusting all at once; the belches of beer-swilling toughs, the soft mewing of kittens, the lowing of mournful calves, rhythmic poundings on a skin drum. There were baby seals nursing, playing with their mother's flippers. They all stared with their huge eyes, deep and rich brown, whiskers framing their soft animal faces. The sounds made in the backs of their throats thrummed through their bodies and out into the ice, along the frozen flatness up through my feet, into my legs and belly.

When it was my turn to jump into the ocean, I stripped naked and leapt high, pulling my legs up in a cannonball, yelling *yahoo!*, and sank so far down that I could put my hands above me and push on the bottom of the ice that was now my ceiling. I paused, smiling, even waving to the photographer, diver Bill Baker, whose flash sent a great yellow flare out into the darkness. How bizarre, to meet him under water like that, him dressed like a seagoing astronaut, camera in hand, taking a photo of me, naked and smooth as a seal under water. I could have been in space. I could have been in some dark, watery womb. The divers were right. For the ten seconds I was enveloped in this strange world, I forgot about the cold. And then I burst again out of the water, propelled by my own desire for air, for life, for light. A hand was there to grab mine as I reached up, a hand that yanked me from the water to standing in one smooth movement, produced a towel, laughed with me, celebrated. It was my birthday and I was born again; born naked, wet and slick with salt, born into the clean and cold, born of ice, born from the most fecund waters in the world.

In the night I jerk awake every few hours, sitting bolt upright in my bed at the Hotel California. Fumbling for my sunglasses, I pull back the curtain to check the weather. Without sunglasses, the clear, bright ice combined with the sun would send a dull ache to the back of my eyes. I see no fog. I dress and go to check the flight manifest on the wall outside McMurdo's galley. My name is on it! But there is something wrong.

"Why do I have the number twelve by my name?" I ask Cindy at the Movement Control Center.

"It's not a number, it's a letter," she says over the phone. "It's an R. It means reserved seat." She laughs. "No, really, it means free ride." She laughs again. I'm being teased all over town. "It's Zen training," a friend reminds me. "You're not there until you are there."

I never do find out what the R means, but I don't care. It's 7:30 A.M. and I'm on the bus, Ivan the Terra Bus, the same one that brought me from the Pegasus airstrip to McMurdo so many months before. The bus is sitting in the dirt outside the Movement Control Center, waiting. No one knows what we're waiting for. Eventually, we drive down the dirt hill onto the ice. On a nicely groomed snow road, we head toward McMurdo's flight terminal. I twist around in my seat to see the front of the sign we've just passed. It wasn't there when I arrived. "Welcome to McMurdo Station Antarctica" it reads, and I watch it fade into the distance.

We finally get on the plane and the plane finally starts taxiing down the ice runway. We stop. My stomach lurches. On board with us are some U.S. senators, some admirals, and a guy with a broken leg. Rob Dunbar, whom I met aboard the *Nathaniel B. Palmer*, sizes them up, then leans over to whisper to me conspiratorially, "We should stay zippered to them. They are what will save us." Just then, the plane engine stops.

We're put back on the bus. On the way from the plane to the terminal, the bus runs out of gas. We can't get out because the door is stuck. The bus eventually gets its gas, and when we're back at the terminal the door does open.

We're instructed to stay in the terminal building, or nearby. We drink coffee and mill around, smoking, gossiping, all trying to

hide our nervousness and impatience. We're all aching with boredom and tension but nothing is happening. "There aren't too many
speeds here at McMurdo," a friend says, wryly.

I call Ruth from the phone in the terminal. I tell her I don't
know if I'll *ever* leave, that I was taken off the plane and don't know
whether I'll be allowed back on. Ruth, who is waiting for me in New
Zealand, is also frustrated. She says with a deep, sincere sigh, "In ten
years maybe we won't care about this."

"Will I know you in ten years?" I ask.

"I hope so," she says.

"How?"

"We'll be waking up beside each other." I feel a flood of warmth
all down to my toes.

Much later, when we're nearly comatose from the combined effects
of boredom and adrenaline, we climb into another C-130, a gray cargo plane with skis. Although we're all supposed to be on this plane,
half of our group is culled out and sent back to McMurdo. Magically,
I am spared. I feel bad for the others, but as we take to the air I sigh
with relief. Dunbar leans toward me again and yells in my ear, over
the engines, that this doesn't mean anything, yet. One year, he says,
he was delayed a week in New Zealand. Every day he and his group
dragged their bags to the terminal, every day they showed up ready
to fly. A few times they got on the plane but had to turn around at
the Point of Safe Return. One time he fell asleep and didn't wake up
until they'd landed. Looking out the window, expecting to see Antarctica, he saw instead green grass—he was back in New Zealand.

When we've been airborne long enough to make us feel we really are
leaving Antarctica, others unbuckle themselves from the red nylon

webbing that makes up the seats of the plane, and find cozy places to curl up among the boxes and bags of cargo. I watch a copilot pull a folding bed down from the side of the plane and fluff up his pillows. I'm envious. I go to the back of the plane, stare out the small round window, and watch Antarctica below me. I see crevasses, like zig-zagged scars. I see the black tips of the nunataks poking out of the icy blanket that covers them. I see curving rivers of glacial ice. I see great expanses that seem to meld into ice, water, and cloud, making it hard to tell what I'm looking at.

As we pass over the land below, I think about naming. I'm not one of the namers of the world, but what if, I wondered, what if I could help map Antarctica; how would I go about that task? As Barry Lopez mused in his writing about the Arctic, "People's desires and aspirations were as much a part of the land as the wind, solitary animals, and the bright fields of stone and tundra." Why not write those desires onto the land? When it's a case of honoring the land, doesn't the heart have as much a right to be on the map as anything else?

What names would I give to the sacred places of Antarctica, places where, for me, momentous events occurred? And what names would I choose for smaller, but no less special features of this land? If I could, I would start my naming in one particular place—75.5 south, 168 east. It was here that I found Ruth again, and finally asked her, in the words of Christopher Marlowe's shy shepherd, to "Come live with me and be my Love, / And we will all the pleasures prove . . ." and she had said *yes*. This would be Come Live with Me Island.

There would be other names for other places. There would be Ghost Story Camp, at the Kiwi A-Frame, for where Ruth, Huck, Chris, and I stayed the night on the ice sheet and told stories into the late hours. Morning Coffee Camp, also known as the Silver City shelter, would stand for the first morning Ruth brought me coffee in bed. There would be Miserable Point (also known as Marble Point), to stand for where I longed for my beloved and sang to her of it over the storm-crackling telephone. There would be Ecstasy Cave, named after the ice cave in Mount Erebus where I was so moved by the vivid, wild blue heart of the glacier. Gifts of Love Harbor would be the new name for Granite Harbor, where I found for Ruth the delicate shell of an Antarctic scallop. Ruth Hills would be the new name for the curving, gracious icefalls along the backside of White Island. Born Again Cliffs would be the new name for Hutton Cliffs, where I dove into the fecund waters of the Ross Sea.

The plane engines drone on. We're past the Point of Safe Return. We truly are on our way! I go up to the cockpit to look at maps, to see where we are. As I enter, one of the pilots looks out the window and points. "That's the end of Antarctica," he says. "Yes," I say, and I wave. Down below the continent falls off into the sea in glacial slopes, and then there is only the gray ocean, where icebergs and floes drift; even from so high above, I see hints of their turquoise underbellies. As we move farther away, the floes break up into smaller and smaller pieces until, under the clouds, I can see only deep blues, with speckles of white here and there. We fly on, crossing over the Antarctic Convergence, the invisible line that encircles Antarctica and its oceans.

Inside this powerful circle, bodies of water and air merge, stirring the world's waters, birthing the world's weather, nursing Earth's ocean life. At the center of the convergence is Antarctica itself, and at the center of Antarctica is the South Pole, where lines of latitude press to a single fine point and rings of longitude converge until they are one—one moment, one mathematical calculation, one singular geographic notation. At this geographic center, outer worlds blend into inner journeys, expeditions and introspections converge, the particular self magically opens out, like an expanding galaxy, to the whole, shared story of the human.

Like the earth waves that the South Pole scientists measure, like the Antarctic currents, the meteorological spirals, the great circling chains of life in the southern oceans, so, too, does the experience of the self echo outward, and then back to us, over and over and over again. The found self becomes the lost self becomes the new self and the new world. This journey is no less than the circling path through the body, to the psyche, on to spirit and back again—an endless sweep of spirals that brings one to the center, where everything must and does converge.

# EPILOGUE

Nearly eight years have passed since I first set foot on the ice at McMurdo Station, Antarctica. During those years, scientific discoveries, changes in political administrations, and the ceaseless tide of people to and from McMurdo have meant changes both for the town as well as for the other U.S. bases in Antarctica and for the continent as a whole. But in other ways, things in Antarctica have remained fairly constant—scientists, tourists, adventurers, poets and explorers are still irresistibly drawn to Antarctica's icy heart; it continues to be one of the least explored places on earth, and one of the most imaginatively provocative.

Science still reigns in Antarctica. Researchers are still studying the hole in the earth's ozone layer; some reports claim the hole is shrinking, others claim it's larger than ever. The fossil remains of two new species of dinosaur have recently been found, and so has the ancient fossilized specimen of a fly. The successful hunt for meteorites continues in Antarctica's frozen hinterlands. Scientists still see in these rocks from outer space the hope of discovering life on other planets.

Drilling is finished at Cape Roberts, but research continues on the 1,500 meters of core that the project's 57-ton drill drew from the ocean floor beneath the Ross Sea. From analyzing the rock, mud, and silt they collected scientists learned that the part of Antarctica they drilled in had a cool, temperate climate with low woodland vegetation and sparse tundra, along with active calving glaciers in the time period from 34 million to 17 million years ago. They also learned that the Transantarctic Mountains became fully formed during this period.

New drilling projects are being planned. Like the Cape Roberts project, they promise to help scientists understand more about climate change in Antarctica and elsewhere. Evidence shows that Antarctica is heating up. One spate of news stories followed the calving of the largest iceberg ever documented when a huge chunk of the continent broke off and was set afloat in the southern ocean, bringing with it renewed fears of the melting of Antarctica and a worldwide rise in sea levels.

Scientists also continue to probe the earth and waters of Antarctica in search of life forms. In one recent breakthrough, scientists managed to thaw out ancient frozen bacteria, giving new life to organisms once thought dead. Some of these bacteria already have been used in patented cures for human diseases and ailments. At the South Pole, scientists with the AMANDA project still look deep into the ice to detect the paths of neutrinos and try to figure out how the earth was born. South Pole telescopes continue to record signs of the big bang, and a new seismic station continues to record the subtle tremblings of the earth.

The enormous effort of science in Antarctica will get a boost in 2007–08, which has been designated the International Polar Year (IPY), when there will be an intense, coordinated field campaign at both poles. The last such scientific milestone in Antarctica was in 1957–58, during the IGY, or International Geophysical Year, when scientists from all corners of the globe converged on Antarctica. On the agenda for the IPY are several broad scientific challenges, including assessing large-scale environmental change, conducting scientific exploration of new frontiers such as the sea floor, and developing new understandings of human-environmental dynamics.

Work on the long-anticipated new station had just begun when I visited the South Pole. At present, a road to the South Pole is being built, fiber-optic cable is being laid to allow better Internet access, and the old geodesic dome is being carted away. In its place, space-aged buildings on stilts will rise, part of the $153 million renovation of the station, which is predicted to be complete in 2006. The new station will have, among other things, a full basketball court and a new hydroponic greenhouse, known as a food growth chamber.

More people than ever seem to be seduced by the lure of Antarctica. Explorers who want to trek across the continent, or some part of it, are flocking to the ice in such numbers that a Web site has been created to monitor their comings and goings. One recent plea asked all explorers to register on the site. Antarctica also has become more popular with tourists who travel there on cruise ships and make day trips to the coast. Thirty thousand tourists visited the continent during the most recent summer season. One news story suggested that, by carrying in foreign bacteria on their shoes, such tourists are the newest defilers of the pristine Antarctic landscape.

Increased commercial activity in Antarctica, including tourism, has come sharply to the forefront of issues being discussed by member nations of the Antarctic Treaty, which protects the continent from ownership by any one nation and prohibits military or commercial use of its resources. The treaty makers are doing crucial work. In 1998, just as I was leaving Antarctica, an environmental protocol went into force that, among other things, established comprehensive environmental protection of Antarctica and banned mining. Among items on the agenda at the most recent Antarctic Treaty Consultative Committee meeting in Stockholm, Sweden, were establishing liability rules for environmental emergencies in

Antarctica, creating a management plan for increased tourism, and developing controls on "biological prospecting."

Despite the focus on environmental concerns, however, some watchdog groups fault the treaty makers for not going far enough. The thirst for oil to fuel the world's biggest economies has already led some prospectors to Antarctica. Another threat that looms is what environmentalists call "bio-prospecting"—or the "mining" of life forms, including microscopic bacteria, which are especially adapted to survival in the extremes of Antarctica. This creeping commercialism is one of the major political issues facing Antarctica.

Soon after I left Antarctica, the National Science Foundation hired a new company to manage services at the Palmer, McMurdo, and South Pole bases. The new contract went to Raytheon Polar Services, a division of Raytheon, reportedly one of the world's largest defense contractors, America's third largest government contractor, and a wealthy contributor to conservative political campaigns.

The new, more corporate culture of the U.S. Antarctic program is sometimes hard for old Antarcticans to get used to. Besides being good humored and community spirited—characteristics that get them through one Antarctic season after another—many of the men and women who've made careers on the ice are by nature individualistic and that, one longtime worker reports, has not been an easy fit with the corporate spirit. During the past presidential election, McMurdo citizens were reprimanded after a photograph of the enormous human sculpture of the Peace Sign they'd created on the ice made it into international news.

The old explorer huts, which for me were richly dense with stories and history, are still being looked after by the Antarctic Heritage Trust. A recently received large grant will allow continuation of their work focusing on Ernest Shackleton's hut at Cape Royds, which the Trust has called one of the one hundred most significant historic landmarks on the planet.

McMurdo is much the same, friends tell me. Still the tacky painted plywood candy canes hung on the utility poles at Christmas time. Still the Skua pile. Still the hydroponic greenhouse (although it might be enlarged soon). The gender ratio of employees at McMurdo is still about 33 percent women and 67 percent men. The galley now has food islands rather than one long line and a stainless steel serving trough. There's a new executive chef, but the old problem of simply getting fresh food to Antarctica hasn't gone away. There's a new science support building. There's a new water treatment plant and a new power plant, but there are still no facilities to harness the power of the sun or the wind.

Some of the people in Antarctica who are part of the stories in this book have stayed on the ice, while others have moved on. Tony Marchetti still keeps watch at Black Island every Antarctic summer. Kim Wolfe, the bread-baker and Black Island cook, graduated cum laude this past May with a degree in anthropology and plans to do graduate research on women's health in Greenland, where she prefers to spend time, although she occasionally returns to Antarctica. She's accumulated sixteen seasons working at both poles. Gerald "Rocky" Ness, the Ice King, left the ice after his fifteenth winter-over and is making a home for himself on solid ground in Northfield, Minnesota. After working in Antarctica for twenty-five years, he isn't yet sure whether he'll adjust to "life in the real world" or "break down and head back to the land of long nights and snow." Don Brogan, who gave me my "underbelly tour" of McMurdo, still works in Antarctica, as does Gary Teetzel, the man who traveled the world with his "possibles bag." Buck Tilley, my tour guide at Cape Royds and on many other adventures, left the ice to work in Africa as a safari guide, and at this writing he's still there. My friend Tom Learned, the photographer whose knowledge of the old explorer huts enriched this book, also has left the ice. Tom now travels back and forth from his home in New Zealand to his new job in Nigeria.

Of all the news from Antarctica during the last several years, the building of the road from McMurdo Station to the Pole has stirred, for me, the most interesting debate, representing, as it seems to, the worst fears of those who still hope Antarctica might remain a special, largely unpeopled and unpolluted open place on earth. A road into the world's last wilderness, one writer has called it, bemoaning its symbolism if not the actual potential for exploitation. The road, which is meant to make it easier to supply the new South Pole Station, will not anytime soon be a superhighway with cars and buses zooming along it. Still, it creates an opening not only for tourism, but also for future commercial activity. On the other hand, a writer for the London *Times* has asked, in relation to the road, whether it isn't time that Antarctica became accessible to more than the "fraternity of the golden," his name for the select few humans who've been able to visit and work in Antarctica. Isn't Antarctica something that belongs to us all, he asked, something for us all to watch and guard?

Ruth and I are still together. Soon after our return from the ice, we spent a week camping and visiting friends in Vermont. One evening, on an island in a special lake in the woods where we'd set up our tent, we took part in a ceremony to celebrate the beginning of our journey together. Ruth and I were going to drive across the continent, from New England to Alaska, and live together in Anchorage.

For our ceremony, we built a tiny boat of birch bark, sealed its seams with pine pitch, and padded its insides with moss, wildflowers, berries and feathers. We set a candle in the center of it all, and then paddled out to the middle of the lake and set our craft afloat. For hours into the night, as we sat on the shore around our campfire, we would glance up and see the boat, still floating, and the candle, miraculously, still aglow. Our journey took us to Alaska and then two years later, back to New England, where we live now, on a large, wooded piece of land, with vegetable and flower gardens and goats.

This summer Ruth and I joined four other couples, three of whom, like us, had begun their love affairs on the ice. We spent the weekend in a small lobstering town on an island off the coast of Maine. In our walks and dinners out and our swims at the local granite quarry, in our small motel rooms, amid much laughter and music and food, our reunion felt a lot like McMurdo. We were close and warm, in good spirits, making due with what we had—good music and friends—and sharing whatever our individual special talents might be (storytelling, singing, playing the guitar, being hospitable—slicing up that delicious cheese or offering a cold drink) for the greater joy of the whole. There was comfort in our connections and remembrances—something more than sheer nostalgia for life on the ice. The comfort might have come from knowing that on the ice we each had played a part in creating community—in creating a culture where people successfully worked together, and shared their lives and imaginations, in a faraway place.

I continue to read stories about Antarctica and am interested in the similarities in these tales—there's the breathless, sometimes confused arrival, the mixed reaction to the cold and the austere beauty, the coming to know the place and the self in the place, and then the heartbreak upon leaving. Many of these tales, especially the personal ones, include a love story of some kind—love for a person, love for the land, or love for some part of a newfound or lost self.

In the news stories I read, I'm taken by how distant and unknown Antarctica is made to seem—how it's still represented as a sensational and alien land from which come Mars rocks, dinosaur bones, answers to the riddles of the universe—a land of mammoth melting ice chunks, roaring winds, and the deepest cold imaginable. The news stories also convey timeless dramas of humans in relation to the solid earth—stranded pilots, scientists killed by leopard seals, South Pole workers whose lives are saved because of surgeries performed via two-way camera between Antarctica and the civilized world, heroic rescue attempts. I continue to meet, sometimes in odd places, other Antarcticans, who—despite differences that might separate us in in our real lives off the ice—seem joined to me, and me to whom I feel joined, just for having been there, just for having been on the ice.

*August 2005, Farmington, Maine*

JENNIFER BAUM

Gretchen Legler is the author of *All the Power-ful Invisible Things: A Sportswoman's Notebook.* Her essays have appeared in *Orion, The Georgia Review,* and *American Nature Writing 1999,* among other publications. The recipient of two Pushcart Prizes, Legler received her PhD from the University of Minnesota. She is an associate professor in the Department of Humanities at the University of Maine at Farmington.

*Toward the Livable City*
Edited by Emilie Buchwald

*Wild Earth: Wild Ideas for a
World Out of Balance*
Edited by Tom Butler

*The Book of the Everglades*
Edited by Susan Cerulean

*Swimming with Giants: My
Encounters with Whales,
Dolphins, and Seals*
Anne Collet

*The Prairie in Her Eyes*
Ann Daum

*The Colors of Nature: Culture,
Identity, and the Natural World*
Edited by Alison H. Deming
and Lauret E. Savoy

*Boundary Waters: The Grace
of the Wild*
Paul Gruchow

*Grass Roots: The Universe of Home*
Paul Gruchow

*The Necessity of Empty Places*
Paul Gruchow

*A Sense of the Morning: Field Notes
of a Born Observer*
David Brendan Hopes

*Bird Songs of the Mesozoic: A Day
Hiker's Guide to the Nearby Wild*
David Brendan Hopes

*Arctic Refuge: A Circle of Testimony*
Compiled by Hank Lentfer and
Carolyn Servid

*This Incomparable Land: A Guide
to American Nature Writing*
Thomas J. Lyon

*A Wing in the Door: Life with a
Red-Tailed Hawk*
Peri Phillips McQuay

*The Pine Island Paradox*
Kathleen Dean Moore

*The Barn at the End of the World:
The Apprenticeship of a Quaker,
Buddhist Shepherd*
Mary Rose O'Reilley

*North to Katahdin*
Eric Pinder

*Ecology of a Cracker Childhood*
Janisse Ray

*Wild Card Quilt: The Ecology*
*of Home*
Janisse Ray

*Back Under Sail: Recovering the*
*Spirit of Adventure*
Migael Scherer

*Of Landscape and Longing: Finding*
*a Home at the Water's Edge*
Carolyn Servid

*The Book of the Tongass*
Edited by Carolyn Servid
and Donald Snow

*Homestead*
Annick Smith

*Testimony: Writers of the West Speak*
*On Behalf of Utah Wilderness*
Compiled by Stephen Trimble
and Terry Tempest Williams


**THE *CREDO* SERIES**

*Brown Dog of the Yaak: Essays*
*on Art and Activism*
Rick Bass

*At the End of Ridge Road*
Joseph Bruchac

*Winter Creek: One Writer's*
*Natural History*
John Daniel

*Writing the Sacred into the Real*
Alison Hawthorne Deming

*The Frog Run: Words and Wildness*
*in the Vermont Woods*
John Elder

*Taking Care: Thoughts on*
*Storytelling and Belief*
William Kittredge

*Cross-Pollinations: The Marriage*
*of Science and Poetry*
Gary Paul Nabhan

*An American Child Supreme: The*
*Education of a Liberation Ecologist*
John Nichols

*Walking the High Ridge: Life As*
*Field Trip*
Robert Michael Pyle

*The Dream of the Marsh Wren:*
*Writing As Reciprocal Creation*
Pattiann Rogers

*The Country of Language*
Scott Russell Sanders

*Shaped by Wind and Water:*
*Reflections of a Naturalist*
Ann Haymond Zwinger